BOLD TRUST

BOLD TRUST

Prepared by TGH: The Good House Ltd.
www.TGHBooks.com

BOLD TRUST

6 STEPS TO UNRAVEL THE LONG-TERM EFFECTS
OF GASLIGHTING, UNAPOLOGETICALLY TRUST
YOURSELF AND HEAL ANXIETY

TRICIA EASTER

To my bold and beautiful family – Marty, Noah, Asher, and Sadie. Together we have found our wings.

To everyone who is living with anxiety. It's time to fly.

FOREWORD

When Tricia asked me to write the foreword to this book, I was beyond delighted and completely honored by this request! Upon reflection, I realized I have a unique vantage point, as I have been working with Tricia for about five years (at the time of writing this), as a support practitioner. Through my work with her, I have had the immense privilege of witnessing the inspirational unfolding of Tricia's journey into *Bold Trust*.

I remember very early on in our work together, I was amazed at how much was being uncovered, discovered and healed! All the internal work Tricia achieved prior, despite having no support, helped make her ripe and ready for long-lasting change. Inside the safe container of our sessions, I was continually in awe of her process into deep and lasting self-empowerment. To this day, I still find it an absolute gift to witness Tricia's ongoing journey of self-excavation and commitment to truth, no matter how challenging it may be. Tricia is living proof that you can overcome anxiety and of what is possible when you are committed to the process that she has so beautifully illustrated throughout this book.

What sets Tricia apart is that not only has she bravely unearthed and faced the source of her anxiety, but she has meticulously written her process down to help anyone else who is suffering. This book leaves no stone unturned, and delves into all aspects of what she has uncovered to be contributing factors to anxiety through her own personal experience. This is why Tricia's book is such a tremendous gift, because it is a result of hard-lived and hard-won lessons. Tricia has intrinsically learned these lessons, and I feel I am one of the few people who can testify to her miraculous journey. I have watched her bravely dismantle old beliefs and rewire her nervous system, which has brought her to the heart-wrenching realization of who actually had her back, and who didn't.

Tricia truly covers every base in this book, with each chapter deep diving into many different facets and layers of what causes anxiety. She lays out her process on how to clearly hear and trust your emotions and the importance of following your intuition regarding food and exercise. Tricia explores the necessity of having spiritual support on your healing journey, and the essentials of how to re-establish your self-worth and value. She fearlessly encourages you to uncover your light and guides you to no longer dim yourself in any way! Tricia helps us to embrace our soul's rhythm, release what is not ours, and to go boldly and bravely into what brings us joy! You will also find exercises, journal prompts, and resources offered throughout the entirety of the book so you can truly integrate this work on the deepest level. All of Tricia's wisdom is poured into this book, culminating in supporting *you* on your unique journey to *Bold Trust*.

I was thrilled when Trica shared that she was writing this book; there is no one more qualified for this much-needed offering. We as a society need this wisdom and guidance more than ever, especially from someone who has truly lived it. I see so much anxiety every day in my practice and have also learned through my own experiences. Tricia has uncovered and shared throughout this book the underpinning of what needs to change for those of us who have suffered or are suffering with anxiety.

I am sure so many people will wish they had this book on their journey, so if you have found it in your hands today, consider yourself blessed!

This book can and will change your life, if you are ready.

Kat WB

Certified Holistic Health and Wellness Practitioner

CONTENTS

INTRODUCTION

"Perhaps the greatest risk any of us will ever take is to be seen as we really are."

— CINDERELLA

Do you find it difficult to make big life decisions or even smaller decisions on your own about things affecting your health, family, or your career? How many times have you asked a friend, teacher, family member, doctor, or co-worker for advice? Do you value their thoughts and opinions above your own? Do you trust them more than yourself?

If you've answered *yes* to any of these questions, then this book is for you. While it's not inherently bad to seek guidance or advice from others, it becomes problematic when you place more trust in them than yourself.

YOU'VE DONE NOTHING WRONG

The most important fact from this book I want you to know, at your core, is that it's not your fault you have anxiety. You've done nothing wrong. You haven't manifested anxiety or mishandled emotions or events in your life.

Anxiety is one of the most misunderstood illnesses and is recklessly approached by family, friends, medical professionals, and alternative health practitioners. Since it's a mental illness, essentially an invisible illness, there's a misperception that you can just stop it. People don't intentionally choose to have anxiety. It's not like you have a magic wand you can wave to make anxiety go away but instead you choose to purposely put away your wand because you *want* to feel anxiety.

Anxiety is an illness, just like any other sickness such as Lyme disease or diabetes. Those who have anxiety need patience, understanding, and compassion too. People with anxiety may be smiling on the outside, but they're experiencing tremendous amounts of suffering on the inside. People who have anxiety need to feel safe so that they can communicate their feelings without derision or judgment. From this safe space, they can then reach out and get the help and support they need, however that support looks for them. Because everyone is unique, what each person needs for support will look different compared to others. Whatever your path looks like, trust it and know it is meant for you.

20 YEARS OF ANXIETY

My personal experience of having anxiety for 20 years left me feeling hopeless and worn out. Even worse, I completely stopped trusting myself. I spent these 20 years searching for answers and placing trust in everyone else but myself including medical doctors, holistic health practitioners, counselors, therapists, nutritionists, acupuncturists, chiropractors, spiritual leaders, friends, and family. I valued their thoughts and opinions over my own. I completely handed over my power to the "experts," even when I sensed they were wrong and let them influence the choices I made and even worse, how I felt about myself. The end result of this misplaced trust was that my self-trust was shattered.

For 20 years, I kept trying to push through my anxiety. I believed that since anxiety was all in my head, I could just ignore it or bypass it. Some of the healing modalities I tried worked for a little while, helping me manage anxiety but never getting to the root cause of it so I could actually heal it. As the years passed, I continued to neglect my own intuition and consequently my anxiety kept getting progressively worse and more debilitating. As trust in myself declined, so did my anxiety.

I didn't trust myself about what foods to eat, how to raise my kids, or even how to decorate my house. This was far from the life I wanted to live. To others I probably seemed like I was doing very well, but I felt like I was drowning as my anxiety got worse. The truth was that I was suffering inside. I was stuck in a vicious people-pleasing pattern, giving away my power and freedom to others.

After living with anxiety for 20 years, when my anxiety was at its worst, I threw a life ring out for myself— something only I could do for myself. At this point, I turned to my spiritual support and surrendered my healing to them. And boy did they step in and lead the way.

Anxiety was the wake-up call for me, raising a red flag indicating that something in my life wasn't working. First, I had to fully release the shame of having anxiety. Then my healing journey required me to examine and reflect on each and every relationship in my life, both personal and professional. I no longer wasted precious time, energy, or money on toxic relationships or in draining environments. Soon after, I began to take center stage in my life, making sure my voice was heard and my needs were met.

Finally, after 20 years of searching for answers on how to heal anxiety, I learned that I had the answers inside me all along. I discovered that I am more powerful and wiser than I thought. I just had to learn to trust myself again.

THE MENTAL HEALTH STIGMA

I was shocked to learn that 42 million Americans suffer with anxiety, according to the National Alliance on Mental Illness. At least 20% of Americans have an anxiety disorder! Anxiety disorders are the most common mental health illness. Furthermore, some studies suggest that during the pandemic anxiety tripled compared to previous years.

These statistics both comfort and sadden me. It's wonderful to know that I'm not the only one who's struggled with anxiety. It's much more common than I thought! Unfortunately, the stigma associated with anxiety and all mental illnesses left me feeling alone and isolated during my hardest times with anxiety.

The detrimental emotional impact of the mental health stigma prevents many people from reaching out and getting the help and support they very much need. Historically, mental health issues have been poorly received and understood. The strong misperception that anxiety is all in your head creates shame in those who have it because it wrongly appears that you are choosing to have anxiety.

It's helpful to discuss the facts and information about anxiety to help release shame for good. By fully releasing shame, you make room for divine healing to take place. Remember that you've done nothing wrong and also that you're not alone. Openly and honestly talking about anxiety gives a voice to those who live with this illness. Truthful and vulnerable discussions about your struggles as well as your successes break down the mental health stigma, releases shame, and allows you to embrace your self-worth, all of which are necessary to heal anxiety.

WHAT IS ANXIETY?

Anxiety is multifaceted. If you do an Internet search for the cause of anxiety, most medical websites will say the cause is unknown. From my experience physical, emotional, and spiritual factors all contribute to anxiety. Rarely is it just one thing that needs to be "fixed" since anxiety is a unique illness that affects your body, mind, and soul. To free yourself from anxiety, all three of these layers need to be addressed so that you can heal deeply and because everyone's anxiety is different, what you need to heal will be specific to you.

Physical

There's a very real physical component to anxiety, just like any other illness. Since anxiety is a mental health condition, many people don't realize there are physical issues that significantly affect anxiety. Healing anxiety requires you to heal your body so that you have the physical strength to also address the challenging mental and spiritual aspects of anxiety.

I've researched and studied holistic health and nutrition for 20 years and have tried almost every diet in an attempt to heal anxiety, leading me to get certified in Personal Nutrition and Sports Nutrition. I have personally had the best results with Anthony William's nutrition information. He recommends fruits, vegetables, herbs, spices, and wild foods to be used medicinally to heal physically, emotionally, and spiritually, all of which have helped me rebuild my nervous, endocrine, and immune systems. In contrast to the conventional medical theory that anxiety is caused by an imbalance of serotonin, a neurotransmitter, in your body, Anthony William states that the real physical cause of anxiety is from a virus or viruses attacking your nervous system and vagus nerve, combined with heavy metals in your brain. While I have had great results with Anthony's information, keep in mind that what works for you may be different. I have more information on my website, angelsgoldhealing.com, that goes into more depth about healing anxiety with nutrition.

Emotional

Personally, it would have been so much easier if I just needed physical healing. If some adjustments to my diet would have fixed it, I would have been better long ago. Even though I tried to heal anxiety just physically, it wasn't enough, and I very much needed to address my emotional and spiritual aspects too.

I see anxiety as an emotional wake up call. Something in your life isn't working for your highest good. Anxiety arises when you lose touch with yourself, when you forget that you have needs and wants. Yes, I said wants because it's very healthy and normal to have wants.

Anxiety is also an emotional response to the dysfunction physically surrounding you. It's perceived that you are the problem because you have a mental health illness, however you're not the problem at all. Instead, it's the people or environments around you that are affecting your mental health. Most people just don't see the dysfunction because it's all they know. The fallout from toxic people and places can unground you, causing anxiety.

Spiritual

When you have anxiety, your soul is crying out to be seen and heard. Your soul needs to shine—it's why you're here. You may have dimmed your light out of fear and you may feel unsafe when you are seen. You may also people please for a false sense of security, further dimming your light. If you don't know your self-worth, you may feel as if you don't deserve to shine even though this couldn't be further from the truth.

Spiritually speaking, anxiety is a sign that there are parts of yourself that you are keeping in the dark. Anxiety is an invitation to bravely step into the darkness and let your light start to spread into every corner of that darkness. There is no bypassing this deep exploration into these parts of your soul. Even though the darkness might seem heavy and scary, once you start shining your light the darkness fades and you then uncover the magnificence of your soul. Your soul is the power behind your voice and your voice is the ticket to your power and freedom from anxiety.

The light that you shine on the darkness is unconditional self-love. Love and fear cannot co-exist because love is stronger than fear, thus cancelling out fear. As you shine your light, you are sending unconditional love to the aspects of yourself that need it the most. By learning to love every single part of yourself, anxiety will heal as love gently hip bumps fear out of the way.

WHAT IS GASLIGHTING?

*"the psychological manipulation of a person usually over
an extended period of time that causes the victim to
question the validity of their own thoughts, perception of
reality, or memories and typically leads to confusion, loss
of confidence and self-esteem, uncertainty of one's
emotional or mental stability, and a dependency on the
perpetrator."*

Gaslighting ultimately destroys self-trust, putting the
gaslighter in a position of power. Gaslighting deceives
victims into no longer trusting their own memories and
perceptions of reality. It is a form of emotional abuse that
exploits people, creating confusion and wreaking havoc
on their mental health. Gaslighting is used to destabilize
you so that you displace trust from yourself to the abuser,
giving them power so that they can control you.

Some forms of gaslighting include lying, denying,
distracting, and blame shifting. You have most likely been
gaslighted extensively in any relationship where you walk
on eggshells, feel unseen and unheard, second guess
yourself, people please, and have lost trust in yourself.

Gaslighting is insidious and pervasive, coming from
different sources such as your family, friends, clergy,
teachers, employers, institutions, and society. All of these
sources compete to create the narrative, and more
specifically, your narrative telling you what you to think,
what types of dreams and goals to have, and how to feel.

Gaslighting can come from therapists too, not realizing that the cause of your anxiety is external to you from the people and places around you—some really close to you.

The fallout from gaslighting and those who gaslight you are what's behind your anxiety. You are not firmly grounded in yourself because you're unsure what your true reality is because of all the gaslighting you've received. This book will help you unravel the long-term effects of gaslighting so that you can find your voice and reclaim your power and that starts with returning trust to yourself.

WHAT IS BOLD TRUST?

Bold Trust is not loud, rude, arrogant, or in-your-face. It's not about proving anything to anyone. **Bold Trust** is a peaceful, self-assured, inner knowing that you're right. Regardless of the chatter outside of you, you know what's right in your own heart. And that's enough. During this lifetime, it's your mind and soul in your body. Only you know what's right for you.

Bold Trust is bravely following your own healing path. Everyone is unique and different, so no two healing paths will look the same. Your individual healing path will be based on your own specific needs and will happen in your own divine timing as you boldly trust yourself that you are on your right path.

Bold Trust is a divinely guided journey. Surrender your healing journey to the divine. Trust that you will be safely guided, and the next steps will be clearly shown to you. When you welcome in support from spirit—God, the angels, the universe, a whole new level of healing takes place. An angelically inspired healing path brings healing to your core, at a deeper level. The guidance of the universe is inside you, therefore trusting spirit is also trusting yourself.

Bold Trust is about finding your voice, reclaiming your power, and fully, unapologetically trusting yourself. Instead of fear and anger, your strength will grow from a space of fierce self-love and self-worth. Your newfound **Bold Trust** will be your North Star guiding you on your own healing path, guiding you to heal anxiety.

Bold Trust comes easily to some people but not most, especially when you have anxiety. Learning to boldly trust yourself is like training for a marathon. You have a training plan (this book), which can be used as a guideline to build and strengthen your muscles and cardiovascular system (intuition) so that come race day, you have what it takes to finish the race (boldly trust yourself). Except you will not just finish the race, but you'll finish strong and exceed your expectations. This is a glimpse of the enormous power and strength within you.

MY BOLD JOURNEY

A few years ago, I lost a good friend and my first dog, Blue, within a month of each other. These losses hit me hard and soon my anxiety flared up. For me, it had to get worse before it got better. It's in these dark moments that all the superficial layers in your life get pulled back so that you can clearly see and hear your soul. Your light shines brightest when you are in the darkest times.

My friend, now on the other side, divinely intervened and started to highlight all the cracks in my foundation. With his help, a new path was shown to me so that I could build a solid foundation to heal anxiety and reclaim my power. With my new strong foundation, I have been able to clearly see my past, present, and future with all veils permanently removed.

My childhood felt very much like the Cinderella story. In the children's tale, Cinderella's ticket to freedom from the abuse and neglect of her childhood is her missing glass slipper. At the ball Cinderella is radiant. She is shining her light and is glowing in her beautiful gown, glass slippers, and styled hair. She is so transformed that her own family doesn't recognize her. Before midnight, Cinderella loses her glass slipper while running away in fear of her whole self being seen. Her fear of being judged or even worse, persecuted, is how she loses the very thing that gives her freedom from the chains of her family. When Cinderella tries on her glass slipper again, she sees how it perfectly fits her because it was made just for her. For me, my glass slipper, my ticket to freedom, was my voice.

Like Cinderella, I also had a fairy godmother, my grandmother, who also happens to literally be my godmother. She was the only one in my family to understand me and I now know we have a soul contract. She died at the age of 102 a week before Christmas. What a gift it was to have her here for so long. Even though she had been ready to die for a decade, it's no coincidence that she held out until I found my voice. After I found my voice, trusted it, and finally used it to free myself, my fairy godmother died the next day. We both got our freedom.

I had to rescue myself. This was and is a journey for only me to make. The hardships and invalidations I endured as a child and for a while as an adult definitely left their mark. However, I broke free and chose not to let my past define me. Instead, I learned from my experiences and became strong. Strength from a place of self-love and self-worth lasts longer and is more resilient than from a place of fear or anger. My glass slipper, my voice, has been my ticket to freedom from anxiety. Before I boldly used my voice, I first had to learn to boldly trust myself.

HEALING BOOK

I wrote **Bold Trust** as a healing book, with affirmations, so healing is ignited in you as you read it. The trusts that I share in the book are written in the sequence that they were revealed to me by my angels. Each trust builds on the previous trust, starting with trusting your feelings and emotions. Take your time reading the book to give yourself the proper time and space to process each trust and see how it applies to your own life.

In each chapter I share techniques that will help you to fully grasp, know, and strengthen each trust within yourself. Try to use any or all of the tools that work for you. You might even discover your own unique method that helps you. I recommend keeping a journal close by as you read **Bold Trust** to help you navigate the exercises throughout the book.

All of the affirmations and life lessons in this book are tools you can use and implement in your own life. These tools will strengthen and build trust in your intuition, the part of you that knows all the answers. Building trust in every aspect of your being not only heals you but emboldens you to live your best and most authentic life. Building a strong trust in yourself paves the way for your freedom from anxiety.

AFFIRMATIONS

Bold Trust is multi-layered, meaning each chapter of the book builds a layer of self-trust. The first chapter, I Trust My Feelings and Emotions, is the most important because it creates a solid foundation for the subsequent chapters. Since your emotions are messages from your soul, trusting your emotions allows you to trust what your soul is communicating to you.

I Trust Myself to Eat and Exercise Intuitively creates a primal trust in yourself. Eating and moving are essential not only for your survival, but also to feel your best. With all of the different diets and fads it's easy to lose touch with your own personal relationship with food and exercise.

The following chapter, I Trust that I am Fully Supported, helps you develop a strong and stable support network that encourages and assists your healing. Welcoming in support from your angels allows them to show you what true support looks and feels like. Anything that is not supportive will hinder your healing and weigh you down.

I Trust My Light is what you need to know without a doubt in your heart. There's nothing you need to do, be, or prove. You are enough. Period. Knowing you are enough helps to pull the roots of anxiety and self-doubt out from you, like pulling weeds out from your energetic body.

The chapter, I Trust the Rhythm of My Soul, came to me in a dream from the divine. It's about dancing with your soul and honoring your soul's uniqueness and divine timing. There's information on following your own path, the path that's right for your soul's growth and nourishment.

I Wholeheartedly Trust Myself is about fully embracing all of the trusts from the previous chapters. It gives tools about how to protect the self-trust you've built so that you can continue to return to yourself. This chapter helps you tie in your newfound **Bold Trust** with finding your voice and reclaim your power so that you can be free from anxiety.

MY PRAYER TO YOU

The solution for healing anxiety is simple and at the same time complex. Trusting yourself to heal anxiety sounds simple, right? The tricky part is addressing all the different aspects of yourself where you have lost trust. For most, the lack of trust and self-doubt is deeply ingrained. You don't even realize you're doing it. **Bold Trust** walks you through each aspect of your life where self-trust needs to be deeply rooted inside of you.

Be patient with yourself as you read this book and apply the affirmations. It takes time for the new patterns of self-trust to become your new normal. Healing takes time. This is a journey, with twists and turns and many new aspects of yourself to see, so be kind and gentle with yourself. Remember that Rome wasn't built in a day but have faith that growth and healing is happening.

My prayer for you is that this book solidifies and strengthens your self-trust so that you find your glass slipper, your ticket to freedom from anxiety. I share the lessons I've learned in **Bold Trust** so that your intuition is restored, helping you remember that the answers you need are inside of you. With renewed self-trust, my goal is for you to reclaim your power, a power that was only ever meant for you and you alone and use it to free yourself from anxiety and live your life boldly. Anxiety is rooted in self-doubt and **Bold Trust** is the opposite. **Bold Trust** starts and ends with you.

1

I TRUST MY FEELINGS AND EMOTIONS

"We cannot selectively numb emotions. When we numb the painful emotions, we also numb the positive emotions."

— BRENÉ BROWN, *THE GIFTS OF IMPERFECTION*

ONE OF THE MOST CONFUSING ASPECTS OF HEALING ANXIETY is understanding, accepting, and trusting your feelings and emotions. My emotions used to terrify me so I actively avoided movies, books, Hallmark cards or anything that would make me cry. Any strong feelings scared me, especially anger and sadness and whenever I allowed my true feelings to show, I felt incredibly vulnerable. I thought that I needed to control my emotions to take control of anxiety and my method of controlling my feelings was to run from them. As an avid runner, I both literally and figuratively ran from my emotions. The stronger the emotion, the further I ran and the worse my anxiety became.

When my anxiety was at its worst, I felt uncomfortable even leaving my house. Everything made me anxious– driving, heights, flying, large crowds, being directly in the sun, and more. I was embarrassed about my anxiety and did my best to hide it. Hardly anyone knew the anguish I felt and those who did know were often judgmental and impatient. My own embarrassment and self-judgement in addition to the judgements from others was like adding lighter fluid to my anxiety, fueling my anxiety and making it worse.

It became a cruel cycle. The worse my anxiety got, the more I hid. The more I hid, the more I lost trust in myself. The more I lost trust in myself, the worse my anxiety became. I completely lost trust in my body and mind. I no longer trusted myself to make any decisions that affected me or my family.

Blocking out my emotions was the catalyst that ignited my anxiety. I didn't know how to digest my feelings, and unfortunately all my emotions got lumped into one big feeling of fear. I was completely out of touch with my feelings and unaware of the impact my emotions were having on my anxiety.

ANXIETY AND YOUR EMOTIONS

Anxiety is an illness that's rooted in emotions because anxiety is something you feel both emotionally and physically. Anxiety and your emotions are also nuanced. For people who have anxiety the thought of becoming friends with your emotions sounds torturous. Anxiety feels like your emotions are on overdrive, making it difficult for you to live your daily life. Since anxiety is incredibly uncomfortable, it's tempting to want to mute all of your feelings because the thought of not feeling anything sounds better than feeling anxiety.

Second, most people don't have a clue what their real feelings are, which is especially true for people who have anxiety. Anxiety is partly the result of having your feelings and emotions gaslighted on both a small scale (family, friends, teachers) and large scale (institutions, society). Therefore, when you're not actively trying to avoid your feelings, you're unsure about what your true feelings are.

TRUSTING YOUR FEELINGS AND EMOTIONS

This distrust and confusion around your emotions is what feeds anxiety, so to heal anxiety you need clarity surrounding your true feelings. Most people don't know how to sit with their emotions and process them because they're unclear about them. It's not something that's respected, admired, or embraced, yet it's the very thing needed to uproot anxiety.

There's also vulnerability in showing your feelings. Being honest about your emotions can feel very uncomfortable like you're emotionally naked, but know that this type of vulnerability comes from your inner strength, strength and confidence from being comfortable in your own skin.

A strength that grows from knowing you're safe embracing your emotions.

I learned that you can't control your emotions, you feel what you feel, and to feel is to be human. The part you can control is your response to your emotions, how to process them instead of running from them. I learned you need time and space to process your emotions, to feel sad, angry, or any other emotion. I learned that your emotions are not a curse but instead are a gift because it's how your soul and the Divine communicates with you. Trusting your feelings and emotions is trusting both your inner and divine guidance that's leading you to freedom.

Bold Trust starts with trusting your emotions. Strong unwavering trust in your feelings is the key that unlocks your healing journey. Below are the three steps to trusting your emotions.

3 Steps to Trust Your Feelings and Emotions

1. Identify and accept your feelings without judging them.
2. Give yourself permission to patiently process your emotions.
3. Practice discernment to determine which are actually your own feelings and what you may have picked up from another person, place, or thing.

Trust in your feelings builds the foundation for the rest of the chapters in this book. Boldly trusting your emotions will safely guide you along your healing path. Let's get started!

Step 1: Identify Your Feelings

Your feelings are meant to be embraced, not feared. All of them. Emotions are at the core of your existence. They are messages from your soul, guiding you to authenticity and integrity. Your feelings are your inner compass, keeping you in touch with your intuition, which is like your own personal North Star guiding you in the night. If you've ever had a bad feeling about something or someone, that feeling is your intuition kicking in saying "no" or sometimes "Hell, No!" to that person or situation. If you keep checking in with your emotions and allow yourself to process them, you'll be safely guided along your healing path and throughout your life. Unfortunately, your true feelings can get obstructed by confusing messages from family and society.

FAMILY MESSAGES

Either intentionally or unintentionally, your parents or guardians and the environments you were raised in programmed messages in you from a young age. Some of these messages may have been helpful, but other messages may be blocking your true feelings and emotions. These messages are ingrained in your subconscious so you may not even realize that they are there. Once you take a step back and begin to see what messages you accepted to be truths about yourself and the world around you, you can reshape and replace these messages with empowering beliefs. You can create new truths that support and encourage your expansion and growth. Just acknowledging any deep-seated disempowering messages is a huge first step.

Here are some examples of unhealthy messages surrounding emotions I heard as a child that may resonate with you.

"You shouldn't feel that way."

"Don't show people how you really feel."

"Just pretend that you're OK."

"Don't be upset. You're tough."

"You're too sensitive."

These messages are confusing and downplay your real feelings. There is no "right" or "wrong" way to feel. These statements are more revealing about the person saying them instead of having anything to do with you. Whether these messages are said out of ignorance or maliciously, they are unacceptable. They shut down who you are. I received many of these messages from a young age and was taught not to trust my feelings or myself. I carried these false truths around with me into my adult life and they became part of my inner dialog, their effects lingering and transforming into anxiety.

Throughout my childhood, my feelings were continually downplayed. Whenever I was emotional my feelings were ignored, mocked, or negated. I was often told that I was tough and shouldn't be upset. Even though this was my parents' narrative and not mine, I adopted it as if it were my own because I didn't know any better. Their invalidation of my emotions made me feel like I wasn't allowed to have, much less express, any emotions. As a result, in adulthood I was completely out of touch with my emotions. I had learned to put them all in a vault. Whenever any emotions did surface, I felt extreme shame–I was supposed to be tough, right?

As a child and as an adult I was also told frequently that I'm too sensitive. I've come to learn that "you're too sensitive" is code for "don't call me out on my bad behavior." Over the years, I've observed that the people who have said that to me are trying to shame me for being upset by their rude actions or comments.

My family of origin is completely obsessed with outward appearances. At some point, after each one of my three children were born, someone inevitably remarked about my weight, my stomach, or anything else about my body that had changed from being pregnant. When I would get upset by these rude offenses, I was told I was "too sensitive." And you know what? I believed them. Not only did I feel devastated by their hurtful comments, but I was ashamed for being sensitive to their harsh words. After doing a lot of internal healing, I now see that their words weren't about me, but were instead about their own insecurities. They were projecting their own feelings of inadequacy onto me. The same applies to when I was told I was tough. They were projecting their fears surrounding their own emotions and vulnerability.

Due to the disruptive nature of any deeply ingrained messages, you need to pay close attention to these messages you've inherited so that you can disempower them and release them for good. You have to be hypervigilant about the words you use and phrases you hear, to not only build trust in your feelings but for your overall confidence too. You have to monitor your inner dialog and consciously and carefully choose your words because your words have power.

Below are some questions to help you determine if a message you've heard is helpful and worth keeping or harmful and in need of reprogramming.

Questions for Decoding Family Messages

- Does the message shame you for your feelings?
- Is the message critical of you?
- Does the message imply you need to change who you are fundamentally?

If you answered yes to any of the questions above, it's time to start reprogramming. Below I have rephrased the negative programmed messages from above into healthy empowering truths.

"You shouldn't feel that way."

"I am safe and secure in all of my feelings."

"Don't show people how you really feel."

"It is safe for me to show my authentic self."

"Just pretend that you're OK."

"I have good days and bad days, and that's OK. In fact, that's life!"

"Don't be upset. You're tough."

"It takes strength to be in touch with my emotions."

"You're too sensitive."

"My sensitivity is a gift."

Take some time to shift and reprogram any family messages you've absorbed, not only about your emotions but also about yourself in general. Consistently shifting any negative messages that have morphed into internal beliefs to empowering messages will reprogram your psyche, allowing you to feel safe with your emotions and to trust them.

SOCIETAL MESSAGES

Society also programs you with many mixed messages around emotions. Just think about how uncomfortable people get when they hear a baby cry. Babies are just expressing their feelings the only way they know how, yet it makes people feel distressed. Maybe it's because a baby's cry holds a mirror to people's own intense underlying emotions that have yet to be acknowledged.

Honestly expressing feelings is seriously frowned upon by many people. Some people take off running at the slightest inkling of emotions and I used to be one of these people. At the same time, people attach emojis to text messages and emails to show emotions that otherwise aren't conveyed by written words.

These mixed messages from society are incredibly confusing. On the one hand, you're encouraged to explore your inner child in order to get in touch with certain feelings. You're told to accept how you feel with messages like "you do you." On the other hand, you're pushed to overcome "negative" feelings with messages telling you to be strong and resilient so you can "beat" how you're feeling. These messages are frustrating because they imply that your feelings are a game, with one set of emotions winning and the other losing. The mixed messages you get from society are extreme and polar opposites, and you could get whiplash if you adhered to them all.

In books and in the media, there are many messages about being positive. There's a misperception that you should strive to feel happy all day every day, just like the song "Don't Worry, Be Happy." These messages are so freaking confusing! To have a positive outlook on life is wonderful. I personally view the world through the 'glass is half full' lens. However, suggesting that because you feel anything other than positive emotions is wrong and means you're attracting negativity in your life is reckless. That puts an insane amount of pressure on you. It also suggests that you are less than if you experience any of the normal uncomfortable emotions.

Social media can be a great space for people to connect and a wonderful resource for healing. However, social media also perpetuates the message of "happiness all the time." Maybe you too have a friend on social media who is constantly posting perfect pictures of their perfect life with a perfect caption. (I know I've been guilty of this too.) It's important for you to know that these posts aren't always true and don't reflect on you, especially if everything in your life isn't "perfect." Just like the family messages above, this type of posting is all about people dealing with their insecurities and their need for validation. These pictures or posts are just snippets of someone's life and not the whole truth.

Social media has often made me feel isolated, especially when my kids were young. After spending the day dealing with dirty diapers, potty training, puppy accidents, and spit up, I would hop onto my social media account to unwind. The snapshots that filled my friends' feeds with their beautifully orchestrated days and their perfectly behaved children left me feeling deflated and, quite honestly, alone. My days looked nothing like what I was seeing, and I felt guilty for having days that did not feel joyous. Eventually, it got me wondering why there is so much stigma related to people being honest about not only their emotions but also their lives. Why do people hide their truths? Is it because of how feelings are labeled? Or is it because many people's emotions have been gaslighted? I believe the answer is a combination of both.

GASLIGHTING AND YOUR EMOTIONS

Family and societal messages that minimize your emotions or try to create a narrative of how you should feel are a form of gaslighting. You and your emotions are gaslighted whenever anyone shames, denies, or invalidates your feelings. No matter the reason behind them, these messages disempower you, steering you further from your truth.

Gaslighting is extremely detrimental for your mental health because it causes you to question your reality. It's a form of emotional abuse that occurs in narcissistic relationships, which I'll discuss more in chapter three. When you are gaslighted, your experiences are denied. Comments such as "you're overreacting," "cheer up," or, again, my favorite, "you're too sensitive" are all examples of gaslighting. Anything that minimizes your feelings and emotions or causes you to question your truth is gaslighting.

Every feeling you have is normal and you never need to justify your emotions. Again, it's been my experience that people who say invalidating comments are projecting their own issues onto you. Your emotions shed light on the emotions that they've pushed aside and that makes them extremely uncomfortable.

Are there moments when your feelings have been undermined? Are you ashamed of any emotions you feel? Do you hide your feelings from friends, family, or anyone else? How many times have you shut down your emotions by permitting other people's rude and often hurtful behavior? These are tough questions to ask yourself and it's even more difficult to answer them truthfully. But you have to be completely honest with yourself and your feelings to get to the root of your anxiety.

HONEST EMOTIONS

To even label your emotions as "positive" or "negative" is unnecessary and harmful. Labelling your emotions is to judge them as good or bad and is damaging your mental health because it eliminates the acceptance of all emotions. I prefer categorizing emotions as comfortable feelings and uncomfortable feelings. Comfortable feelings include a lot of fun emotions such as love, excitement, and joy. Uncomfortable emotions are the less fun ones such as anger, frustration, sadness, and overwhelm.

Learning not to judge your emotions is a game changer. Instead, recognize which emotions feel like cozy blankets and which ones feel like sandpaper. Remember, there are no negative emotions and that uncomfortable emotions are indicators of where you need to nurture yourself more.

True strength and resilience come from being open, honest, and vulnerable with your emotions. How you experience the world through your emotions is what makes you unique and human. Your feelings are the fabric of who you are. I used to think that being labeled as "emotional" was an insult however, I now see it as a compliment because it demonstrates both courage and compassion.

When it comes to emotions, your soul wants you to be honest with yourself, to be clear about how you're feeling and what your intentions are. If you're unsure, that's ok too. Be patient and give yourself time and permission to sift through your feelings. The more honest you are with your emotions, the easier it is to process and let go of the uncomfortable ones. Below are some questions to help you become more honest with your emotions.

Honest Emotions Questions

1. Are you judging your own emotions?

2. Do you feel guilty when you feel like you're having a bad day?
3. Do you feel conflicted around the holidays if you don't feel joy all the time?
4. Do you hide your true feelings for fear of being judged?
5. Do you fear attracting negativity in your life if you feel perceived "negative" emotions?

If you answered yes to any of these questions, you are having difficulty being honest about your emotions. Know that you're not alone. These messages from family and society are deeply ingrained. With that said, you can begin to untangle these messages and create your own truths. While comfortable emotions such as joy feel great in your body, it's the uncomfortable ones like anger and sadness that lead you towards personal growth. If you find yourself battling with your feelings or are confused about your emotions, remember the following three steps to get in touch with your honest emotions.

Honest Emotion Activation

1. Tell yourself that all your feelings and emotions are ok and give yourself permission to feel your emotions.
2. Remind yourself that there are no negative emotions.

3. Write down in your journal at least five feelings and/or emotions you're experiencing at that moment.

These steps help you to tune into your body, allowing you to experience your feelings safely and freely. Understanding the impact of the messages you've received from family and society that have infiltrated your own beliefs is the first step to **Bold Trust**. Deprogramming yourself from these destructive messages creates space for you to begin to embrace and welcome in all of your emotions, without judgment so that you can process them.

Step 2: Process Your Emotions

Anything other than accepting your emotions for what they are is avoiding them, whether you're actively running from them or pushing them aside. The truth is you can't push past your emotions. Here's what took me a long time to figure out. When you push away your feelings and emotions, you get stuck in those emotions and never fully process them. These feelings get trapped in your body.

Unprocessed emotions are like a messy brew in a witch's cauldron—an emotion concoction. When you continually push your feelings down, they don't disappear but instead become your personal witch's brew, your own emotion concoction, a concoction that ferments and churns and gets bigger until it overflows and leaks out. This is what happened to me. I had so many emotions stuffed into the cauldron that they fermented into anxiety. Things that wouldn't give other people anxiety spurred panic in me because my body had no other way to process the emotions.

A well-lived life includes the full spectrum of emotions. However, being present with your uncomfortable emotions can feel overwhelming at times due to their intensity. Tools to properly process your feelings will help them move through you so that they don't get stuck in your body, alleviating some of the overwhelm. The steps below outline how to process your emotions so that you can fully embrace all of your feelings instead of running from them.

PROCESSING YOUR EMOTIONS - 3 PARTS

Follow this three-step procedure to process your emotions.

Part 1: Isolate Your Emotions

- Scan your body and identify where you actually feel the emotion in your body. Do you feel it in your gut, heart, or shoulders? There's no wrong answer to where you feel any given emotion in your body. Everyone will feel each emotion differently.

Part 2: Feel Your Emotions

- Find a quiet place to sit and focus on the emotion and where you feel it in your body.

- Practive deep belly breathing. Take deep breaths with your belly expanding every time you inhale. Envision and feel your breath moving into the part of your body where you're experiencing the emotion. Continue this breathing exercise for five to 10 minutes or as long as you need. Often times people take short shallow breaths when they experience pain, causing these feelings to get stuck in your body. Many of your intense emotions can feel painful, so it's important to remember to breathe deeply to process and move the emotions.

Part 3: Tools and Techniques to Work Through Your Emotions

After you have tuned into your body and feelings, one or more of these tools and techniques will further help you to process any uncomfortable emotions you're experiencing.

- **Quiet and/or alone time.** This is not selfish. In fact, it's required so that you can tune out distractions and focus on yourself. Time to yourself creates space for you to be present in your feelings.
- **Meditate.** The art of meditating requires you to be present and engaged in your feelings, allowing you to fully process them.
- **Journaling.** Because your words have power, putting your feelings and emotions onto paper is incredibly healing and freeing. Writing about your feelings and the events surrounding them is an emotional release so that you can process and move them.
- **Creating.** Everyone is creative. Doing something creative engages your senses and takes you out of your mind for a while and into your heart, which helps you to unlock emotions that are deep within.

- **Walking in nature.** Physically moving while tuning into your emotions will help them to move through and out of you in combination with the healing effects of spending time in nature.

I also learned there is no mandatory time limit on processing your emotions. Really sitting with your emotions can feel awful. Sometimes it feels so intense and lasts longer than we want it to so you might worry you're going to feel that way forever, but these emotions will move through and out of you. My mantra during these difficult times is "this too shall pass." Uncomfortable emotions really do move on if you give them the amount of time they need to cycle through. Please be patient with yourself.

When I first began to build **Bold Trust** within myself, I had to come to terms with the truth that a holistic counselor I saw had invalidated and gaslighted me for 20 years. (I will talk more about her later in the professional support section below.) I completely trusted her and stopped trusting myself and generously gave my power away. When I began to follow my own truth again, I felt very angry with her. (Anger is my least favorite emotion and feels very uncomfortable for me.) At first, I felt guilty for being angry with her and tried to internally justify her poor counseling skills. After I moved through the guilt and into the anger, the anger felt so strong that I thought it would consume me and be there forever. During this time, I took many walks in the woods in my backyard to help process my anger. For weeks I felt this intense anger, but as I continued to be present with this anger and take walks in nature it eventually started to dissipate. I learned that my feelings of anger were not only normal but necessary. Acknowledging my anger and processing it taught me about boundaries and never giving my power away again. It began my journey to trusting myself.

ANGER AND SADNESS

Intense emotions such as anger and sadness are completely normal feelings and have a purpose. It's essential for your mental, physical, and spiritual health to be present with these emotions. While they may feel very uncomfortable in your body, they are shedding light on issues in your life.

The anger I felt towards my holistic counselor is the perfect example of anger having a good purpose. That anger showed me where I needed boundaries in my life, boundaries where I prioritized my own intuition instead of valuing other people's thoughts and opinions, solid boundaries so that I never handed over my power again.

Anger is very misunderstood in society. The emotion itself is not bad, but it's how people express it that causes trouble. Anger is necessary for growth and healing, surfacing when boundaries have been crossed. Identifying and strengthening your boundaries is mandatory for healing, which I discuss more in chapter six.

A very healthy way to process anger is by moving. Run, jump, swim, hit a punching bag, let out a loud scream, just let it out. Anger is a lot of uncomfortable energy running through your body, so it's best to move to help release it (however, remember that you can't run FROM it, but you can run WITH it to give it a release).

Another helpful technique for processing anger is letter writing. Handwrite a letter to whomever you are angry with and don't hold back. Let it all out in the letter and feel free to use harsh words and after you have let it all out, burn it. This ritual has amazing results, burning away the anger energy in your body. It will take time for your body to process anger, but both of these practices help to take the edge off.

Sadness is another uncomfortable emotion that can stem from a wide range of situations such as disappointment or loss. Sadness is also a very normal human emotion and moments of sadness in your life are natural. Crying is an excellent way to process and release sadness and there is no shame in it. Sometimes it feels like once you start crying the tears will never stop, but they do. Shedding tears is very cleansing and sadness is a necessary emotion to help you heal.

If you are in the midst of processing some intense and powerful emotions and you feel overwhelmed, it's OK to give yourself small breaks. A funny TV show, light-hearted reading, or walking with a close friend are healthy ways to give yourself a small reprieve from the discomfort you're feeling. It's important to be clear with yourself that these are not tools to be used to distract yourself, but to give yourself a break to catch your breath. Small breaks can help intense emotions feel less overwhelming.

PROFESSIONAL SUPPORT

Enlisting the help of a support professional is an effective option for help with processing your emotions. It's an opportunity to be seen and heard and to create space for profound healing, whether it's a therapist, counselor, life coach, or any other healer. Trust yourself and choose someone whom you feel is a good fit for you.

Among some healing professionals there is a perception that you can control your emotions, allowing you to control anxiety and no longer be affected by it. I strongly disagree. This kind of thinking lays the groundwork for people to judge their emotions and the emotions of others. It also sets the stage for anxiety sufferers to feel like failures because they aren't "controlling" their emotions properly, further exacerbating anxiety. It's another ingredient added to your emotion concoction. The whole idea of controlling your emotions is impossible. You can control how you express your emotions, but you can't control what you feel. Ultimately, these mental health professionals are gaslighting their clients.

The counselor I used to see told me that whenever I had strong and intense emotions such as anger, frustration, or fear, I should allow myself 10 minutes to feel them and then simply move on. She applied this 10-minute rule to any feelings she deemed "negative." But for some reason she didn't apply this rule to sadness. I suppose in her mind, sadness was a more acceptable emotion.

I can't even begin to explain how detrimental this type of counseling was for my mental health. First, to judge my emotions and then to suggest I shouldn't feel any strong "negative" emotion like anger for more than 10 minutes. All feelings and emotions are normal and acceptable, and they can linger for more than 10 minutes. These counseling sessions left me feeling invalidated and destroyed any trust in myself that I had before I sought out support.

Any type of professional support that invalidates people's feelings and emotions, and sometimes intense emotions is reckless. These "support" professionals are trivializing people's emotions and their lives. Healing anxiety is about giving yourself time and space to process your emotions, not control them.

All healers, whether they are a therapist, counselor, or life coach, need to adjust how they view and treat clients with anxiety. These fields see anxiety as something that's inherently wrong with the client who has anxiety (thus the perceived need to teach them to control their emotions). Even though anxiety is felt internally by the client, these professionals should instead address what is external to the client that has either caused the anxiety and/or feeds it.

Earlier in the chapter I discussed how gaslighting causes people to distrust their own reality, adversely affecting their mental health. The mental health community needs to have more of an awareness of the dynamics and effects of narcissistic relationships. Instead of further gaslighting their clients, coaches and therapists need to validate their clients' emotions and give them tools to process their feelings, so that their clients can trust themselves instead of handing over their trust to others.

I have wasted too many years and too much money on ineffective and detrimental counselors, therapists, and holistic healers. Growing up in a dysfunctional family, I had no clue what good support felt like. I gave my power away to these professional support people thinking that they were the experts because I desperately needed help to alleviate my anxiety.

When you find someone who truly supports you and your mental health, profound healing will occur. Again, it all comes down to trusting your feelings and intuition about who you choose for professional support. Below, I'm passing onto you what I learned about finding good professional support.

> *"The best teachers are those who show you where to look, but don't tell you what to see."*
>
> — ALEXANDRA K. TRENFOR

A good coach or therapist will help you navigate your experiences and emotions through your own lens. Unfortunately, some misguided healers and therapists think they are the expert about you. They try to twist and bend your vision to see your own life events through their lens. Good professional support will set you in the right direction but won't give you the answers. A good healer will see each client as a unique individual and will support each client's unique healing path.

A good counselor should **never** be critical of you. Ever. Again, their role is to support you—your imperfections and all. They are paid to hold space for you to support your healing, not tear you down. Holding you accountable for your actions is good, but it can go too far. The counselor I saw enforced accountability so much that I began blaming myself for every argument or miscommunication in my life.

Remember, that even though a counselor might be an expert in their specific field, you're the expert about yourself. If at any point it doesn't feel right, it's time to move on and find someone else. Whoever you choose to be your support should help build trust in yourself, not break it down. While healing doesn't happen overnight, if you don't start to see improvements or feel better over time or if you in fact feel worse, it's time to change. This goes for any and all services including but not limited to therapists, counselors, holistic practitioners, chiropractors, acupuncturists, nutritionists, or life coaches.

Step 3: Discernment

W hat if some of the feelings you experience aren't yours? What if some of the anxiety you feel isn't your anxiety? What if some of the anxiety you experience is intense feelings, energy, or even anxiety from another person, place, or situation? Knowing what is yours and what isn't provides a lot of clarity around anxiety, helping you understand that some or most of the anxiety you feel was never yours but instead comes from the people and environments near you.

Discernment, in the context of this book, is the ability to distinguish what is true for you, more specifically, discerning which emotions are yours to process while releasing any feelings that aren't yours. Just acknowledging which feelings and emotions are yours keeps you centered in yourself, allowing you to detach from all that isn't yours.

EMPATHS

I took a year off from seeking out any kind of professional support after my terrible experience with the counselor I saw for 20 years. Discontinuing my patient/client relationship with this counselor was the first **Bold Trust** decision I made. As you know, during that year I processed a lot of anger and then something extraordinary happened—I started to hear my own intuition and voice again. Trusting myself and using my intuition, I found an incredible holistic support practitioner to further support my healing. Choosing to work with her was the second **Bold Trust** decision I made on my journey to free myself from anxiety.

During one of my earliest sessions with my new support practitioner, I learned that I was an empath. Even though I had been involved in the holistic health community for 20 years, I had no clue what an empath was. However, learning I am an empath gave me clarity as to why I had anxiety. What I discovered is that because of who I am, I pick up on and easily feel what's going on all around me. I feel other people's emotions, and at times, other people's physical symptoms. If I don't protect myself, crowded places deplete me because I feel everything and everyone. I'm very sensitive and need a lot of alone time to replenish my energy and to feel centered. If you're an empath, you may be especially sensitive to the energy surrounding you, which will significantly impact your anxiety if you're unaware of your sensitivity.

Empaths have the unique gift of picking up on emotions experienced by other people and energy from places, things, and situations. It's as if they have a special antenna that's able to read feelings and emotions. Like smoke detectors, they are feeling detectors except instead of detecting fires, they detect energy and emotions. They also easily absorb energy and feelings from other people and places which becomes pretty sticky when dealing with anxiety. If you've ever been told you're too sensitive or have felt that way about yourself, most likely you're an empath.

Are You an Empath? Questions

Below is a list of questions to ask yourself to determine if you're an empath.

1. Are you sensitive to sounds, light, sensations, and smells?
2. Do large crowds drain you?
3. Are you drawn to nature, animals, and babies?
4. Do you have a strong desire to help people?
5. Are you unable to watch scary or violent TV shows or movies?
6. Do you need a lot of quiet alone time to recharge?
7. Are you prone to overeating to deal with emotional upset?

If you answered yes to most of the questions above, you are an empath, and there's a good chance that a lot of the anxiety you feel is not your own. This means you may be absorbing other people's intense and strong emotions, or even their physical feelings and mistaking these as your own.

Types of Empaths

In Dr. Judith Orloff's book *The Empath's Survival Guide*, she lists three types of empaths:

1. **Emotional Empaths** – You absorb other people's feelings and emotions into your body

2. **Physical Empaths** – You feel other people's physical symptoms in your body
3. **Intuitive Empaths** – You have an incredibly strong intuition and pick up on energy from other sources

You can be one type of empath or all three. You might have a strong connection to animals and can receive information about their feelings or insights about them. Maybe you receive telepathic information about people, places, or situations. You may also be strongly connected to plants, nature, and the earth and may experience sensations that afflict the planet. Perhaps you're a medium and can receive messages from spirit.

I'm a combination of all three types of empaths. I'm extremely connected to spirit and frequently receive messages. I feel other people's physical symptoms, especially if I'm emotionally or physically close to that person. I'm strongly connected to the earth, in particular to trees. I also pick up on other people's emotions. While I've had to learn how to discern between what is mine and what belongs to someone or something else, I've come to see that being an empath is a gift. It's an extra sense—a sixth sense. Being an empath means you have extra insight into the people and the world around you, allowing you to make informed decisions for yourself and your healing path.

EMPATH PROTECTION

If you are an empath, you have probably been made to feel like something is wrong with you for being sensitive, perceptive, and just different–for being yourself. As a result, your self-worth has taken many hits. As an empath, you are also more prone to anxiety and exhaustion because you are constantly outside of yourself, feeling everything, which is why you need to recharge frequently with plenty of sleep and alone time.

Your empathic sensitivity is a gift. You know when you walk into a room what the emotional climate is and can respond accordingly. However, there are steps you can take to protect yourself and your sensitivity. The first step is practicing discernment. Discerning what is yours to process and what isn't is life-changing, especially when healing anxiety.

Pay attention to how you feel around certain people and places. If you notice an uncomfortable feeling inside you that seems to just have sprung up, it probably isn't yours. Tune into yourself to see if this feeling is in fact yours or from someone or something else. A simple prayer saying, "I only want to feel what is mine" will clear up anything you may have picked up. Observe how you feel after saying this.

The second step is to shift your attention from outside yourself to inside of you. I can't stress enough how important it is that empaths come back into themselves, get grounded, and become centered. What this means is that as empaths, since it is easy to be drawn out of yourself, it is crucial to establish daily self-care rituals that return your energy back to yourself and keep it there. To heal anxiety, you need to tune into yourself and your own feelings in order to process them so that you aren't confusing someone else's feelings as your own.

Since you are "outside" of yourself and overly accommodating, you can be an easy target for narcissists who are eager to take advantage of your kindness and generosity. I talk more about narcissists and the impacts of their behavior, especially on empaths, in chapter three and chapter four.

EMPATH PROTECTION PRACTICES

Below are some spiritual practices that will return your energy back into yourself. Your energy will not only come back into you, but if you do these practices routinely, your energy will stay rooted in you, making discernment easier.

1. Grounding Exercise

Grounding keeps you connected to the earth. This connection to the earth helps to reduce overall stress levels and keep you centered. You can visualize roots growing out of your feet, meditate about connecting your energy with the earth, or try anything else that connects you with nature. It can be taking your dog for a quiet walk at the beach, fishing, hiking, or swimming in a lake or an ocean.

Here are some more suggestions for ways to become grounded.

- Touch or hug a tree
- Walk barefoot in nature or just your yard (called Earthing)
- Enjoy a sea salt bath (mimics ocean water)
- Swim in natural bodies of water – lakes, oceans, streams
- Take a walk in the rain
- Visit or plant a garden
- Listen to birdsong
- Focus on your breath
- Feel the warm sun on your face

2. Energy Protection Practices

Energy protection is invaluable. To put it in Star Wars lingo, you're reinforcing a force field of energy around you that protects your energy and prevents energy from other people or any other sources from getting through to you. Getting in the habit of doing energy protection takes practice and dedication. I highly recommend it daily.

Praying to and connecting with Archangel Michael is a powerful protection practice. Archangel Michael is the angel of protection who can help clear your energy field and remove all unhealthy energetic cords you may have. Cords are energetic attachments to people, places, or things that are holding you back. Waving a crystal selenite wand along your body while also praying and visualizing cords being cut by Archangel Michael is especially powerful.

Say this simple prayer to Archangel Michael to welcome in his support and protection:

Archangel Michael and angels of protection, I welcome your love and support. Thank you for guiding me and protecting me from all unsupportive energies. Thank you for gently holding me inside your bubble of protection. I am safe.

Feel free to use your own words and prayers that feel right to you. Kyle Gray's book, *Angel Prayers*, has additional prayers to Archangel Michael and the other Archangels.

3. Connecting to the Moon and Moon Goddesses

The moon's energy is strongest during a full moon. Full moons help to shine a gentle soft light, a glow, on your emotions. Full moons activate all of your senses, especially your emotions and feelings. The moon and full moon cycles are symbolic of the feminine cycles, causing the moon energy to be spiritually revered as feminine because of its cyclical nature and connection to emotions. The feminine energy of the moon is present in all humans, both men and women, and animals.

Many cultures have a goddess deity they associate with the moon. For example, there's Artemis, the Greek goddess of the full moon; Ix Chel, the Mayan moon goddess; and one of my favorites Diana, the Roman moon goddess. The moon goddesses I find most helpful are

Archangel Haniel and Freja, the Norse moon goddess. They help you to fully understand your emotions and discern what is yours. Archangel Haniel brings your emotions out fully into the light so that you can see their beauty and view them as gifts. Freja helps the mist in your life to lift so that you can cut through illusions to see the real picture. When you are able to see the truth of what is actually transpiring in your life, good and bad, you are better able to trust your emotions, intuition, and discernment. If you feel like you could use the moon goddesses' support in your life or would like to just connect with them, pray to them and welcome their help.

The full moons and the moon goddesses offer pathways to become in sync with your intuition and to trust it. Intuition is really all about feelings, insights, and hunches you get. Therefore, the precursor to trusting your intuition is trusting your emotions.

4. Crystals and Orgonites

Crystals are tools you can use to protect your energy and to energize yourself. You don't need a huge hunk of rock–something small enough to carry with you is all you need. Crystals are not only beautiful to look at but have healing abilities too. My two favorite crystals are amethyst and moonstone. Amethyst represents transformation and healing. Moonstone, as the name suggests, is associated with the moon and enhances your connection to your emotions. During a full moon, place a moonstone crystal on your windowsill to charge with the moon's energy.

Keep your moonstone near you whenever you want to be more in touch with your emotions and intuition.

Clear quartz crystals are wonderful too and absorb any negative energies while balancing energy. Clear quartz, when paired with another crystal, will enhance its abilities. Rose quartz enhances the energy of love, whether for yourself or someone else. Obsidian is another great crystal that protects you from negative energies. Orgonites are also great to have as they protect your energy and assist you in healing. Orgonites are a combination of metals, crystals, and minerals, protecting you from electrical and magnetic fields (EMFs) and other negative frequencies.

I place crystals near me during meditations to enhance my connection to the divine and ultimately myself. If I'm feeling drained, I place crystals on my chakras to absorb and remove any negative energies and to help me recharge. In my office and all the bedrooms in my house, I have clear crystals in all four corners to clear and balance the energies in each room. Everyone in my family has an orgonite beside their beds and I have one in my office. I always wear either an orgonite necklace or a crystal necklace for energy protection, too. It's important to remember to place your crystals and orgonites in the sun to cleanse them and in moonlight, especially during a full moon, to charge them.

THE HUMAN EXPERIENCE

It is human nature to experience emotions. It's the whole point of life; it's why you're here. Yes, you're sensitive. Yes, you're emotional... and it's a gift. Celebrating your emotions will allow you to fully appreciate your ability to have extra insight. Your feelings and emotions are your perspective about your life experiences and is unique compared to others.

Completely accepting and embracing your emotions will transform your healing. Fully stepping into your emotions and feelings teaches you how to discern between what is yours and what only ever belonged with others. Consistently surrounding yourself with protective energy and emotionally soothing practices will help to calm your nervous system, giving you some relief from anxiety. Being patient and giving yourself time for emotions to move through you will ease your anxiety as well.

As a long-distance runner, it took me a while to realize that processing my emotions (and healing in general) just takes time. It's not a marathon. You won't finish sooner if you run harder and faster. However, moving through your emotions can be similar to an endurance event. The divine has no set timeline for how long it takes for certain emotions to pass. It will just take time, so keep moving. Trusting your feelings and emotions is the necessary first step to discovering your own healing journey. Once you fully embrace how you intuitively feel, you can trust that you're on the right path.

I n the following chapter, I discuss how to trust yourself to eat and exercise intuitively. Both food and exercising fuel and strengthen your body and are necessary to not only survive but to thrive. The skills you learned in this chapter will help you to trust your body's signals and cues. Eating and exercising intuitively further strengthens self-trust and removes another layer of anxiety.

2

I TRUST MYSELF TO EAT AND EXERCISE INTUITIVELY

"I am careful not to confuse excellence with perfection. Excellence I can reach for; perfection is God's business."

— MICHAEL J. FOX

THE POWER OF GOOD NUTRITION IS CAPTIVATING. I'VE SEEN and heard many inspiring stories of people who have healed themselves with nutrition and a healthy lifestyle. Caring for your body with good nutrition and exercise lays the groundwork for powerful healing to transpire. Thoughtfully nourishing yourself strengthens your physical body so that you are able to delve into the more challenging emotional and spiritual aspects of healing anxiety.

When I was in my early 20s, a medical doctor referred me to a holistic nutritionist to help with my anxiety. The doctor told me there was nothing more the medical community could do for my anxiety, which was unsettling to hear at that age. I was unsure what to expect before my first appointment with the nutritionist, but I left my session loaded with information and supplements. At first, I was overwhelmed with all of the new information I received about what I could and couldn't eat and what was healthy and unhealthy. Food and eating as I knew it was over, but I was completely on board because of the possibility of having relief from anxiety. I felt like Neo in *The Matrix*, except that I had accidentally taken the red pill. I never went out searching for the red pill but stumbled on it while searching for help with anxiety.

My experience with this kind of nutrition was mixed, however. While I felt better eating healthily, I started to not trust myself, especially my body. This was the beginning of my 20-year cycle of not listening to my body or my intuition. I started trusting the holistic nutrition "experts" more than myself. Every time a new physical symptom came up, I looked outside of myself for answers and grew more uncomfortable with my body. I lost trust in my body and felt like it was failing me. I now know that each new physical symptom was my body giving me clues about the dysfunction going on in my life. I just wasn't listening.

Exercise also changed for me. I stopped listening to my body about what exercise worked for me and instead I listened to all the external voices around me. As a lifelong runner, my exercise of choice has always been controversial. When I first got involved in the holistic community 20 years ago, running was always criticized and ridiculed for being too strenuous. Even today there is still a lot of talk in different nutrition and exercise communities about running being an ineffective form of exercise, especially for weight loss. Rather than physically doing what I loved and what felt right to my body, I started to do intense rigorous workout plans instead. My workouts started to feel like actual work and were no longer fun and carefree. I eventually stopped looking forward to my workouts and began to dread them.

Both food and exercise became too structured and rigid for me. There was no flexibility. There was no listening to my body. Even worse, there was no joy. There was only pushing and manipulating. Rest was also something I did not prioritize and unsurprisingly, my anxiety got worse.

With my knowledge of nutrition, I could dedicate an entire book talking about healthy eating and exercise. However, most of us already know or have an idea about nutrition and exercise and there's already a ton of information available in books and online. I recommend doing your own research and drawing your own conclusions about what exercise and nutritional plan is best for you. Instead, I'm going to talk about the emotional, physical, and spiritual impact of trying to eat and exercise perfectly. Then I'll discuss what it means to eat and exercise intuitively and introduce steps to start listening to your own body's nutrition and exercise needs.

GASLIGHTING YOUR BODY

When you lose trust in yourself due to the long-term effects of continual gaslighting, you no longer trust your body, which trickles down to not trusting what you eat or how you choose to exercise. You may feel more comfortable seeking answers outside of yourself from health and fitness "experts" rather than listening to your own body and observing what works for you. Rigidly applying nutrition and exercise regiments that are designed for the masses only sets you up for failure because there is no one diet or fitness routine that works for everyone. Like fingerprints, everyone is unique.

Ignoring your body's cues is essentially gaslighting yourself. For example, if you keep eating apples even though you feel sick afterwards just because apples are supposed to be healthy, you're gaslighting yourself. Yes, apples are healthy...for most people, but they're not working for you. Restoring trust in yourself involves listening closely to what your body is telling you and adjusting accordingly. Restoring trust in what you choose to eat and how you exercise is part of restoring a primal trust in yourself that gets you in touch with some of your most basic human needs.

PERFECT EATING AND EXERCISING

There is a wealth of positive health benefits that result from healthy eating but like most things, "healthy eating" can be taken too far. As health and wellness has become more mainstream, there's an enormous amount pressure to eat perfectly. What people eat has become a status symbol. People get so caught up in the labels (vegan, paleo, keto) that they forget to check in with themselves and see how these foods actually make them feel. It's great to have a social network to support your nutrition goals as long as you don't lose sight of why you started to eat healthfully to begin with–to feel good and heal.

There's a lesser-known eating disorder called orthorexia that is becoming increasingly more prevalent. Orthorexia develops when healthy eating is taken too far and becomes an obsession. It has physical, mental, and social impacts. Physical effects include unintended weight loss or malnutrition. Someone with orthorexia is completely consumed with healthy eating and they become mentally distracted, unfocused, and unable to function in other areas of their life. A person with orthorexia eventually becomes more and more socially isolated because they no longer take part in social functions or gatherings where they don't have control of their food. The strong desire to eat, not just healthfully but perfectly, is incredibly stressful. This added stress creates extra adrenaline in the body, which has its own set of adverse effects which I will discuss later in this chapter. Orthorexia is an example of when healthy eating becomes extreme.

Eating perfectly isn't healthy and is both extreme and unattainable. It's nearly impossible to eat perfectly. Striving to eat so that you are completely in compliance with whatever set of rules you have adapted saps all the pleasure out of eating and replaces it with stress. Many nutrition and exercise regimens have become militaristic, dictating every food that enters your mouth and every movement your body takes. What you eat or how you exercise should not be structured so that you no longer enjoy eating and dread moving.

TOO MUCH STRUCTURE

Nutrition and exercise plans aren't inherently bad, especially if you have dietary restrictions. In fact, they can be helpful and effective, but there needs to be balance. A good workout plan gets people moving and helps them achieve their fitness goals. However, too much structure and pushing in your workouts causes you to ignore the subtle (and sometimes not so subtle) clues from your body that you're doing too much which can result in an injury or burnout. Likewise, a good nutrition plan sets the stage for incredible healing to occur but taken too far can halt healing or worsen your health.

During my healing journey when my anxiety was at its worst, I was diligent about eating perfectly in accordance with the rules I was given so that I could heal. I was working so hard to get some much- needed relief from anxiety. After about a year of being vegan and eating according to the rules, I had a brief feeling go through me. A feeling of being tired and exhausted from eating "perfectly." A voice in my head said, "Enough!" This feeling freaked me out and I pushed it aside. I had devoted 20 years to studying health and nutrition, searching for the perfect diet. I didn't understand where this feeling was coming from, and I felt that I couldn't turn my back on nutrition. However, this feeling returned and was stronger each time. Eventually, I could no longer ignore the exhaustion I felt. At this point, my healing from anxiety had stalled and wasn't getting better. It seemed like I was stuck.

I slowly started to relax with my nutrition. I began to bring more foods back into my diet, like meat. A vegan diet just wasn't for me at that time. I started enjoying going out to eat with my husband and family again. If the restaurant didn't cook my food with the right oil, I knew I would be fine or if other ingredients I had previously been avoiding, like corn or butter, were in my food, I no longer panicked. The funny thing is my healing started to pick up speed again, and my anxiety started to improve dramatically. I began to see how the stress from trying to eat perfectly was taking a toll on my body.

I had taken things so intuitive and natural as eating and exercising and turned them into something lifeless. It became clear to me that this is not how I was supposed to be living. This is not what God wants for me or you. The divine wants you to enjoy life and the sweetness that comes with it. The angels want you to enjoy your occasional indulgences without guilt—to enjoy and savor that cupcake, or slice of pie, or that low intensity sunset walk with your family or friend. Soak in these events because the bulk of your time is spent in these simple moments.

I also learned that when it comes to introducing a new nutrition plan or implementing a new diet, particularly when herbs or supplements are involved, less is more. This is especially true for people with anxiety. Picking a few things and doing them well is more effective than adding a lot and changing your diet overnight. This applies to other areas of your life too, in addition to diet and exercise. Implementing too many changes at once makes you feel overwhelmed and creates adrenaline.

ANXIETY AND THE ADRENALINE CYCLE

A vicious adrenaline cycle is beneath the surface of your anxiety illness. Too much adrenaline is highly toxic and corrosive to your body. Adrenaline is created by your body to combat stress, anxiety, overwhelm, and other intense emotions you feel. When you worry about eating perfectly, you're adding more adrenaline to your already adrenaline-flooded body, fueling and strengthening the adrenaline cycle that's already set in motion.

When you feel anxious, your body produces adrenaline. The information in the book *Medical Medium* by Anthony William explains how viruses (Epstein Barr and strep) and heavy metals in the body are the root cause of anxiety and other health issues. The adrenaline your body creates then feeds the virus that's attacking your nervous system and makes the virus stronger, subsequently creating more anxiety and more adrenaline.

Constantly pumping out adrenaline also depletes your adrenal glands, which is why adrenal fatigue and anxiety usually go hand in hand. When your adrenal glands get exhausted, they are no longer properly regulating hormone production. Some signs of adrenal fatigue include muscle weakness, increased energy at night, interrupted sleep, blurry vision, feeling dizzy when you stand up quickly, and craving salty foods and stimulants.

The hormonal imbalance caused by adrenal fatigue is another factor that breaks down trust in yourself. Too much adrenaline in the body destroys dopamine in your brain. Dopamine is a feel good neurotransmitter that regulates your moods. This means that when you have a stressful event, the next day you feel a low when your body is out of its reserves of dopamine. If you are constantly in a state of anxiety, you may begin to think that this new low is your normal state of being. Operating from this "low" state will not feel good and can cause you to start doubting yourself more. If you think you have adrenal fatigue and want to learn more about it, read *Medical Medium* by Anthony William. He has an entire chapter dedicated to adrenal fatigue.

All the healthy food in the world can't undo the effects of adrenaline. Eating perfectly can protect you from the negative health effects of adrenaline only up to a point. I don't want you to worry about having stress in your life. Stress happens to all of us and at times it feels out of control and overwhelming. But you don't need to add the stress of eating perfectly to the mix. This is one stress you can let go of.

A big part of healing anxiety physically is breaking the adrenaline cycle. Unfortunately, the stress people put on themselves to eat perfectly negates a lot of the health benefits from good nutrition by creating extra adrenaline. The stress and overwhelm of the expectation to eat perfectly creates conditions for anxiety to perpetuate and worsen.

MANIPULATION

Eating and exercising are also employed to manipulate your body. By manipulation I mean trying to push or control your body to look or perform in a certain way. Manipulating your body with food and exercise is so deeply ingrained in our culture that most people don't even realize they're doing it. Extreme diets and exercise are mainstream and you're encouraged to endlessly push your body. Most people want six-pack abs. Or they want to be highly productive 12 hours a day, seven days a week. Is it worth it though if it's making you sick?

By themselves, I don't think caffeine, sugar, alcohol, or intense exercise are bad. In moderation, they can be effective. When they become a crutch instead of a tool we occasionally use, you are manipulating your body. When you use them to override your feelings, they adversely affect your health. You're using them to trick your body to keep going and performing while forgoing rest. Proper nourishment for your mind, body, and soul is then neglected.

Caffeine

I've seen many people and athletes manipulate their bodies with caffeine (myself included). For some people, it inhibits their appetite so that they eat less. For others, caffeine is used as an extra boost of energy to complete a vigorous workout. I'm not talking about a cup of coffee at breakfast, but caffeine being used to get through your day.

Caffeine provides false energy for your body. If you don't naturally have the energy to complete a workout, listen to your body and perhaps do a less strenuous one. Caffeine produces extra adrenaline in your body that feeds and strengthens the adrenaline cycle that is present with anxiety and further depletes your adrenal glands.

Sugar

Sugar is another food used to manipulate your body that is similar to caffeine. If you're feeling groggy or in an afternoon slump, it's easy to reach for a cookie to give you that extra boost to get you through the day. However, that sugary treat really just gives you an energetic boost for the next 15 to 30 minutes and then you feel more tired than you were before (or if you're like me, you immediately feel the sugar crash). The refined white sugar in cookies decreases your attention span too. Like caffeine, sugar is used to push your body even though you're fatigued, rather than savoring it as the occasional treat.

Alcohol

How many times have you seen a TV show, commercial, or meme about a woman needing a glass of wine after a hard day with the kids and/or work? I'm not personally against alcohol in moderation, but when it's used to manipulate your body as a form of self-medication, I don't find it to be beneficial. After a stressful and adrenaline-infused day, something like a warm bath would help your body to relax more effectively. Unfortunately, alcohol just adds to the adrenaline and is a short term fix for stress.

Instead, it's time to start listening to what your body is telling you. If you're using any of these foods as a way to manipulate your body to do more or keep going, you'll have more serious health problems down the road. Using foods like sugar, caffeine, and alcohol to manipulate your body is like putting a band-aid on a problem instead of addressing the core issues. Pushing your body with sugar and caffeine is an indicator that you're tired and need to rest. Using alcohol is a signal that you need to address the stress in your life.

Over - Exercising

Over-exercising places your body under an incredible amount of stress. This also produces more adrenaline in your already adrenaline-saturated body. Exercising and movement is a great tool to help reduce anxiety, but it can also be taken to extremes.

Like orthorexia, where perfect eating becomes an extreme, there is such a thing as exercise addiction. Exercise addiction wears down your physical body, specifically your musculoskeletal system, and more subtly your immune and endocrine systems. Exercise addiction adds to the adrenaline cycle, depleting your adrenal glands and perpetuating anxiety.

There needs to be balance with eating and exercising "perfectly" so that you stop abusing your body. You need to reframe how you see food and movement. I used to manipulate my body, and my anxiety worsened. I relied on caffeine to get out of bed and sometimes to get me through a long run. As a self-proclaimed cookie monster, I've done my fair share of eating sugar to get me through sleepy afternoons. I used to drink a glass of wine at the end of stressful days when my kids were young to dull my emotions. I've also over-exercised in hopes of getting washboard abs after having three children. These forms of manipulation worked initially, but they didn't last. While I didn't do these in extremes (well, maybe I did with cookies!), my intent was to push my body and override its signals. If you use food to push yourself, let's take a look at how you can nourish your body instead.

Nourishment

"You have to feed your soul!" said a friend I was visiting on a college break as she was stuffing yet another donut in her mouth, not even a good Krispy Kreme donut, but a knock off one from the grocery store! This was her response when I mentioned I was trying to eat healthier. At the time I thought this person was crazy but now I think she was on to something. Hear me out...

When you think of nutrition and exercise as nourishment, it shifts your perception of how you move and what you eat. The word nourishment brings your emotional and spiritual health into the equation in addition to your physical health. It's about feeding the body, mind, and soul. Nourishment brings you back to wholeness. If eating and exercise becomes too methodical, you are not being nourished. It lacks a fluidity and softness that is necessary to heal and to be healthy in general. Nourishment is about going with the flow and giving yourself room to be human. What you need one day will be different from the next day, depending on the external circumstances surrounding you in addition to internal changes and shifts in your body. Being in tune with yourself will allow you to adjust and adapt to these changes. You won't always have it right and that's OK. Just as long as you keep tuning in, listening, and doing your best, you'll be on track.

I recently watched *Eat, Pray, Love* again and was reminded of how vital it is for me to tune into my senses and enjoy eating and to have fun with it. When I was younger, I traveled to Italy just like in the movie, and I observed how their culture embraces and appreciates food. Their food truly nourishes them physically, mentally, and spiritually. Because they eat mindfully, savoring every bite, food and eating are joyful experiences. In Italy, meals are social events, bringing together family and friends. There are multiple studies that show how eating meals together at the table strengthens relationships, proving that the bonding that occurs during social meals provides emotional nourishment.

Nourishment is about enjoying and savoring your food and embracing meals and snacks. Take a minute before you grab a snack to listen to what your body needs. Does it want a sugary snack or is it craving rest? If you still want a cookie or piece of cake, then enjoy it guilt-free. Eating that treat occasionally is nourishment too, but if done all the time it becomes manipulation and a crutch.

Nourishment is about prioritizing rest instead of pushing your body, giving your body a chance to recuperate and recharge. Rather than eating a donut at the office during an afternoon slump, grab a piece of fruit and get some fresh air. Instead of drinking coffee to fuel you during spin class, listen to your body, do lighter exercises, and get some more sleep. Nourishment is essentially self-care coupled with self-love.

Nourishment Ideas

- Take a nap
- Go for a walk
- Take a bath
- Meditate

- Sit in sunlight for five to 10 minutes
- Dance
- Listen to music
- Write in your journal
- Get a massage
- Take an art class
- Cook creatively

I do believe you need to feed your soul, but not with a whole box of donuts like my friend did. The occasional treat won't hurt you. In fact, I think it's good for you, but if you're going to indulge make sure it's *really* good.

INTUITIVE EATING

Eating is one of your most primal instincts. At a minimum it sustains you and keeps you alive—you have to eat in order to live. At best, you feel balanced with sustainable energy. Food converts to energy and supplies you with the nutrients you need to live a good life. Healthy food is medicine and can heal you physically, emotionally, and spiritually. Eating well enriches your life and allows you to feel your best. The gift of health is priceless.

Eating and exercising intuitively requires flexibility to make room for when life steps in. You must have flexibility for when you're sick or even just feel run down. It's important to be flexible with yourself when you have sleepless nights staying up with your teething toddler or even if you want to indulge in that piece of cake at your friend's wedding. Flexibility will allow you to enjoy and take advantage of the beautiful weather and go for a nice hike instead of a full-blown workout at the gym.

Everyone's body is unique and different, so what you need with respect to nutrition and exercise is different than everyone else, and varies each and every day. There's no diet or exercise plan that's suited for everyone. The one thing that does work for everyone is listening to your own body and intuition. I've been studying nutrition for 20 years and there's always a new diet plan and exercise regimen that promises results. It's not bad to listen to what these new programs have to say, as long as you are the expert about yourself. You can try fad diets, I certainly did. Just remember to listen to your body and be your own judge.

WHAT IS INTUITIVE EATING?

Intuitive eating is about taking a moment to tune into your body and listen to what it's telling you. It's about paying attention to how you're feeling and any symptoms you may have. What foods sound more appealing to you? Are you eating that salad for lunch because that's what you're supposed to eat or because that's what sounds good to you? Are you eating that chocolate as the occasional treat or to power you through the afternoon?

Intuitive eating is about doing your best. Forget about what everyone else is eating and do what's supportive of you, your body, your lifestyle, and your budget.

FOUR STEPS FOR INTUITIVE EATING

Follow the steps below to begin eating intuitively again—
to feed your body what it needs and to feel safe and
comfortable in your body.

Step 1: Keep It Simple

Meal prep, meal plan, and cook easy meals—
whatever you need to do to keep your stress
level low. Eating healthfully does not need
to be complicated. Also, healthy eating doesn't have to be
expensive. There are many options to make healthy eating
easy and affordable.

In the past, I spent hours every day in the kitchen
preparing healthy gourmet meals for myself and my
family. It's not bad to spend hours in the kitchen cooking
if that's what you enjoy, but I craved more down time to
relax and invest in my own hobbies and interests.
Eventually, I started making easier meals to free up my
time. I started cooking basic meals like tacos, chili, and
even pancakes for dinner. I just swapped in healthier
ingredients. I discovered that my family preferred the
simpler meals over the gourmet meals I had been making,
and I'm thrilled about the time I freed up. My kids and
husband have become more involved with the cooking too
and are building their cooking skills. Enlisting my family's
help has also freed up more of my time.

There are other options if you're too busy to cook or don't enjoy cooking. Consider an affordable prepared meal service where you pick up or have prepared meals delivered which you heat up. Healthy takeout is another option. To integrate healthy eating into your lifestyle, keep it simple so that it's sustainable.

Step 2: Observe How You Feel Before and After Meals

Before and after you eat, for both meals and snacks, tune into your body to see how you feel with the foods you're eating. These observations will give you clues about what foods are working well with your body. For example, I've learned through a lot of experimentation with different diets that too much raw food doesn't work for me. I don't feel full after eating it, which makes me anxious, further exhausting my adrenals. However, I know that a diet of raw foods works for many other people. Intuitive eating is about finding what's right for you. There is no wrong answer.

Intuitive Eating Exercise

For at least three days (but preferably for a week), keep an intuitive eating journal. You can find a sample worksheet on my website angelsgoldhealing.com/bold-trust that you can download and print or you can use any notebook. Record what you're eating for breakfast, lunch, dinner, and snacks throughout your day. Observe and write in your journal how you feel before and after each meal or snack. Below are some questions to ask yourself to develop intuitive eating:

- What foods sound good to you?
- How do you feel after you eat?
- Do you feel energetic?
- Is your energy sustainable?
- Do you feel full after you eat? Bloated?
- Are you still hungry?
- Do you feel tired or lethargic after certain foods or meals?

These questions help to create an inner dialogue with yourself surrounding food. You'll start to pay attention to how certain foods make you feel. You'll observe if you feel tired or sluggish after a meal or if you feel energized after a snack. Getting to know your body and how it responds to food gives you insight into whether you need to make any changes in your diet. Honoring how you feel about food further strengthens your self-trust, so that the thoughts and opinions of others will no longer influence how you choose to nourish yourself.

Also pay attention to and jot down in your journal any foods you crave during your day. Food cravings are very different from eating what sounds good to you. A food craving is when certain foods keep interrupting your thoughts and you become laser focused on that food. Food cravings aren't necessarily bad. They are your body telling you that it needs something like comfort, rest, or maybe connection with others. You can identify which cravings are good for you and which ones aren't by observing how you feel after eating these foods. As you begin to correlate how you feel after eating certain foods, you'll crave less of the foods that make you unwell because your brain will begin to associate that food with feeling bad and you will start craving the foods that are better for you.

Step 3: Bring Back Joy

It's time to bring joy back to cooking and eating. Before preparing your meal, take a moment to let go of the mindset that cooking is a chore and shift your thinking to see it as a creative outlet. Bring back your childlike joy and play with your food. Be passionate about your food and cook the foods you love, making healthy versions of your favorite comfort foods. Engage your senses while you're cooking and eating and enjoy the aromas, the textures, and the tastes, making cooking and eating fun again. Set some fresh flowers on your dining room table and listen to music you enjoy while cooking.

These are just some suggestions, so feel free to incorporate your own style of fun in the kitchen. No worries if you don't enjoy cooking; you have options, too. You can buy healthy takeout or purchase your food from a meal prep service or even your local grocery store. But still bring back the joy—enjoy your dinner with lighted candles or have a picnic (indoors or outdoors). With the stress you're exposed to everyday, you need to make it a priority to counteract it with joy. Meals and eating have the potential to nourish you in so many ways. How can you bring more joy to cooking and mealtimes?

Step 4: Do Your Best

D o your best and leave it at that. No guilt, no what-ifs, no worrying. Your best is always changing, too. Maybe you're traveling and your best is the healthiest takeout you can get. Maybe you've just had a baby and your best is just having the time to eat a meal. Or maybe you've started a new job with long hours and your best is a healthy frozen meal. All of these are good. Your best is all you can do, and your best is good enough. Actually, I take that back. Your best is awesome! Give yourself a pat on the back and know you're doing great.

Good nutrition creates a solid foundation to support healing anxiety, restoring your nervous system and adrenal glands. Healthy nutrition heals and strengthens your physical body so that you are able to explore the heavier emotional and spiritual aspects of your healing journey. You also just feel better when you eat well—you have more energy and vitality. Emotionally, you feel good about yourself, knowing you're choosing healthy options and making your health and wellbeing a priority.

Yet give yourself permission to be human too. If you've had a busy day and want pizza for dinner, get it and enjoy it! Pizza is your best bet in that moment, and that's perfectly fine. You can clean up your diet the next day. Too much pressure on yourself to eat healthy can make you feel worse.

INTUITIVE EXERCISE

Exercise is a wonderful tool for managing anxiety. Exercise produces endorphins (the feel-good hormones) and reduces stress and anxiety levels. Aside from the physical and mental health benefits of exercise, there are spiritual benefits too that include moving and clearing out stagnant energy from your body.

Many people lose sight of the fact that exercise isn't just about weight management. Exercise and movement are crucial for your health. It strengthens your heart, muscles, and bones, gets the blood flowing in your body, and pumps blood and oxygen to your brain. When you move, the different systems in your body get moving too, such as your lymphatic, endocrine, and nervous systems. A healthy lifestyle that includes exercise helps your body function and move better as you get older. A healthy weight is part of a healthy lifestyle, but many people tend to focus too much on their weight and not enough on their overall health.

THREE STEPS FOR INTUITIVE EXERCISE

Intuitive exercise, like intuitive eating, is about tuning in and listening to your body. It's learning what kinds of movements are best for your body. It's making exercise a priority, while simultaneously prioritizing sleep and rest. It's finding the right balance for your body, between moving and recuperating.

Step 1: Just Move (Every Day) - No Judgments!

S top comparing yourself to others. (This applies to all other areas of your life too.) Comparing yourself to others or even your younger self only sets you up for failure. You never know what's going on behind closed doors, and you don't really see the whole picture. As I've already mentioned many times in this book: everyone's body is different. Your genetic makeup, background, and lifestyle is unique compared to others.

When I was younger, I often compared myself to other runners and athletes in general. I wanted to be faster or run more miles like other runners. Other times I compared myself to athletes with beautiful abs, most who had never been pregnant but some who had. I kept pushing myself more and more to be like other people, instead of just doing my best and accepting myself.

As I got older, I also kept comparing my body to my younger body. After healing some running injuries and taking some time off from running, I was incredibly hard on myself when I started running again. I kept comparing myself to how I ran before my injuries. Being hard on myself and comparing myself to others (and my younger self) held me back. The motto above (Just move every day, no judgments!) is what got me moving again. I focused on what I could do. I have periods of time where I mainly walk and when I'm feeling well enough, I may get a run in. Every day, I check in with myself before deciding which exercise I'm going to do. Listening to my body has helped me maintain my energy and avoid further injuries.

If you're feeling well enough, just move (preferably every day) without judging yourself. Focus on being present, doing your best at that moment, and know that your exercise is good enough. If you're bedridden, your best may just be getting out of bed for a shower. For others, your best might be walking to the end of your driveway. All of these are OK and should be celebrated. Focus on your best right now and release all judgments.

I discussed in chapter one how many people with anxiety are empaths, making them sensitive to the energy around them. Exercising moves the energy in your body. When you exercise, you move any stuck energy through and out of you. If you're dealing with any strong emotions, exercising will help your body process your feelings. Moving energy through and out of you also improves your quality of sleep. Daily movement is nourishment for your body.

Step 2: Balance

As I mentioned earlier in the chapter, over-exercising creates extra adrenaline in your body. When you have to use caffeine or any other stimulant to get you through a workout, your adrenal glands take a hit. If you feel the need to use stimulants before exercise, most likely your adrenals are already exhausted and are left even more depleted after a strenuous workout fueled with sugar or caffeine.

Instead of choosing to manipulate your body, choose to nourish your body with exercise. Exercising is very healthy, but we live in a society of extremes and for many people exercise has become synonymous with pushing. As a runner who lives with a family of athletes, I know that pushing your body is fine to a point. It's OK to push a little to reach your goals. However, if you push too hard, you become depleted. Pushing to an extreme doesn't give your body enough time or resources to fully recuperate.

Observe how you feel both during and after a workout. It's good to be tired after a workout, but you should still be able to function comfortably. Make sure you also schedule time to rest and recuperate. Just as exercise is healthy for us, so is recovery!

Step 3: Keep It Fun!

Most importantly, make sure your exercise of choice is fun. The more joy you have doing it, the more you look forward to it and the easier it becomes to prioritize it every day. The more fun you have exercising, the less likely you are to overdo it. When my running became too intense and I was pushing too hard, I lost the original joy I felt when I ran. Running used to be fun and helped my stress, but it became a chore and created more stress. I took a break from running and started to do less structured activities like walking and hiking. Eventually, I started running again, but this time I set aside my running watch and ran for fun.

To exercise intuitively, observe how you feel before you exercise, during your exercise session, shortly after you exercise, and 24 hours after you exercise. On my website, angelsgoldhealing.com/bold-trust, you can find an intuitive exercise worksheet similar to the intuitive eating one. Below are some questions to ask yourself to help develop intuitive exercise:

- Are you looking forward to doing your choice of movement or are you dreading it?
- Are you fatigued afterwards? To what degree?
- Are you in pain before, after, or during exercise?
- Are you sore afterwards? For how long?
- Do feel energized after your workout?
- Do you have energy to get through the rest of your day?
- Are you reaching for sugar or caffeine to fuel your workouts or to help you get through the rest of your day?

While it's normal and good to feel some amount of fatigue after exercising, you should have enough energy to get through your day without fueling yourself with sugar or caffeine. While some soreness can be good and can promote muscle growth, being sore for more than three days is too much and not only suggests damage to the muscles, but it also makes it much less appealing to do that workout again. I disagree with the "no pain, no gain" approach to exercise because it encourages you to take exercise to the extreme and abuse your body. If you're looking forward to your workouts, you're more likely to exercise. If you don't enjoy it or are in too much pain, exercise will feel like torture, and you will be more prone to skipping it.

The American Heart Association (AHA) recommends 150 minutes a week of moderate intensity exercise and two days a week of muscle strengthening. That's about about 30 minutes a day, five days a week of moderate exercise, such as brisk walking, biking, swimming, dancing, yoga, or hiking, and two days a week of strength training, including weights, resistance bands, and yoga. The AHA also recommends moving more and sitting less overall throughout your day to prevent a sedentary lifestyle.

Walk, ski, hike, swim, dance in the living room, use hand weights or resistance bands, skip, or do yoga. Do whatever sounds like fun to you. With all of the other stresses in our life, bring joy back to exercise and move every day. No judgments!

INTENTION

After studying and experimenting with nutrition and exercise for 20 years, I've come to see that a healthy lifestyle is all about intention, meaning that if you truly believe something is healthy for you, then it is. You can drive yourself to exhaustion researching all the different fads and recommendations (I certainly have). The truth is you just have to do your best, especially with healing anxiety, when the less is more approach is more soothing to your nervous system. What's best for you will be different than what's best for me or what's best for your friend. If you believe your food choices are healthy, then they are.

Picking up fast food for dinner and mindlessly eating while binge-watching TV is not eating with intention. However, picking up healthier takeout for dinner once a week to give yourself a break from cooking and doing dishes while having a movie night with the family has a much different intention. Both are essentially the same thing, while the second scenario has clear and healthy intentions.

Food prepared with love and joy nourishes your body more too. The time and energy used to prepare a meal is a beautiful intention. If you cook a meal for yourself, your family, or a loved one out of necessity but mostly out of love, this meal will nourish them more than any other takeout or store-bought meal. If your budget or schedule dictates that you can only make a box of macaroni and cheese for dinner, I still believe this will nourish you (and hopefully you can still throw in some peas or broccoli). However, if you approach this same scenario with guilt or pressure, then your meal will be lacking.

Pay attention to how certain foods make you feel and make any necessary adjustments but let go of the need to do it perfectly. Trust what your body is telling you because you know your body best. If you believe your nutrition is healthy, then it is. Trust yourself.

3

I TRUST THAT I AM FULLY SUPPORTED

"Accept me at my strongest, support me at my weakest."

— *MALIKA E. NURA*

YOU DESERVE UNWAVERING SUPPORT. SOLID SUPPORT THAT will always be there for you during your best and your worst moments. True support sees the best in you, listens to you, and honors your authenticity. Trusting that you are fully supported is both comforting and healing.

Healing anxiety requires support just like a house needs support. A house is symbolic of your life journey, your soul reclamation. First and foremost, you need a solid foundation that can bear the weight of your healing and growth, which I cover in chapter four. Your foundation is your self-worth and self-love. Then there are the load-bearing columns that further help to support and distribute the weight of your house. You can have as many or as few support columns as few you want. Each column is someone or something that is supporting you, your healing, and your soul growth.

The first half of your support comes from spirit. The divine, God, the angels, and your loved ones in heaven all love you and support you unconditionally. Know and trust that they are here for you, always. You just need to consciously invite them to support you, otherwise they cannot intervene without your permission.

The second part of your support is emotional and physical support: people and situations that support you (for better and for worse); people who uplift, cherish, and celebrate you as you are today; and supportive environments and situations that nourish you and promote your growth and healing.

I love reading articles and memoirs about successful people. It's inspiring to read how many people have overcome adversity to later achieve great success in business, relationships, and personal healing. The common thread in all these success stories is that these people had a solid support system, even if it consisted of just one person. These success stories are a testament that anything is possible with support.

But these stories also made me feel sad. Not everyone comes from supportive families and environments. What does this mean for those who don't have support and may not even know what true support looks like or feels like? While healing my anxiety, I quickly discovered that you can create your own solid support network that meets your needs. The first step in building your support system is welcoming the support of God and the angels.

SPIRITUAL SUPPORT

Something magical happens when you invite your angels to travel your healing journey with you. Fully welcoming and trusting your divine support deeply heals you at your core. When you're knee deep in anxiety, it feels like you're constantly putting out fires, quelling your fears, and are on high alert, anticipating your next bout of anxiety. In this heightened state of fight or flight it is hard to find the quietude and introspection to identify what needs healing in your life. When it feels like your world is always in flames, you may miss the warning signals and directional cues from your body and intuition. This is where trusting your divine support comes in.

It's instrumental for your healing to invite your angels and the divine in to support and guide you. Your angels' vision is crystal clear, unfiltered, and without lenses. Their vision is much better than 20/20, allowing them to see through all the layers of self-doubt and confusion, to target exactly where you need help and support.

Trusting your divine support is a twofold process. The first aspect is opening yourself up to trust the divine and your angels in order to receive their unconditional love, support, and guidance. The second part is trusting your divine support enough to allow them to guide you to build a solid support network that will support your healing and growth.

Trusting the angels and their support is a game changer for healing anxiety. Divine support is so powerful that it's step two in the Twelve Step Alcoholics Anonymous program in which participants state they "believe that a Power greater than ourselves could restore us to sanity." When you're in the midst of anxiety, the core issues you need to heal are hidden under layers of dysfunction, confusion, and gaslighting. Trusting your divine support and their guidance brings your deep core wounds out of the dark shadows of your life and into the light so that they can get dressed with love and finally heal.

YOUR SPIRIT TEAM

I want to talk about your divine support or, as I call it, your spirit team. Your spirit team functions just like any other support service such as tech support or customer service for any product or service. Your spirit team is here for you. Whenever there's an issue, concern, or even when you just want to touch base, your spirit team is here for you 24/7. Whatever is on your mind, bring it—there is no issue too big or small for them.

Your spirit team is here to support and guide you. They love you unconditionally and want the best for you. Welcoming their love and support will take your healing journey to a whole new level and uncover the beauty and depths of your soul. Even when you feel like your healing path has taken a detour and the terrain feels harsh and craggy, you are always supported 100 percent by your spirit team, and they will never leave your side. Trusting in their support and guidance gives you the assurance that you're on the right path even though at times it may feel like you're not.

You get to choose who is on your spirit team. It's completely up to you whom you want in your spiritual corner. Your team can be however big or small you want it to be. It can be God, the angels, ascended masters, or friends and relatives who have crossed over and are now in heaven. I recommend two books by Kyle Gray that go into detail about the different archangels and ascended masters to help you decide who you want as part of your spirit team—*Angel Prayers* and *Divine Masters, Ancient Wisdom*. Read through these books or similar ones like them to help you piece together your spirit team and connect with the energy and wisdom to which you are drawn. Once you know who you want on your team, consciously invite them to support and guide you by writing their names down under the heading "spirit team" on a piece of paper, praying to them, or just having a conversation with them thanking them for their support.

GUIDANCE

The angels are desperate for you to know that you don't have travel your path alone. Trusting your spirit team means knowing that they are always with you. Asking for and receiving help from the divine is not a weakness. Even though opening yourself up to the divine can make you feel raw and vulnerable, know that you are safe and divinely protected. Surrender, trust, and vulnerability are all part of your relationship with the divine.

You don't have to know what your entire healing journey will look like. Trust in your spirit team means that you will be guided to the next step you need to take. Afterwards, the next step will be shown, as well as all the steps after that. Your spirit team is always walking by your side, guiding you as to which turns to take. Parts of your path will be easy and fun, while other parts will be hard. All of these parts are for your soul's growth and will heal anxiety.

Surrendering your healing to the divine requires you to release the tight grip you have on the reins of your life. Anxiety for most people is about control, usually as a means to avoid pain. Surrendering to the divine means being aware of what you can control and releasing what you can't to God and trusting you are in good hands. Opening yourself up to be vulnerable takes courage and inner strength. It's your vulnerability that allows you to hear the messages and guidance coming through for your healing.

Trusting your divine support can look like saying no to someone or something even when on paper everything looks good. It's trusting the messages and guidance that say not everything is at it seems at first glance. As you trust the divine and yourself, you'll dig a little deeper and see that you and your support team were right and you will feel more confident about your decision. Other times, trust in your spirit team will mean following all of the clear "yes" messages that are coming your way.

Your spirit team and the divine try to communicate with you in many ways. It's normal to initially feel a little uncertain about the messages you may be receiving. There is no right or wrong way to get messages from the divine and there is no set standard of communication that applies to everyone. The best advice I can give is that if you think you're getting a message from the angels, your spirit team, or a departed loved one, you are. Trust your intuition and fully receive the message. Sometimes it's guidance pointing you in the right direction, other times it's healing energy you're meant to receive (this is especially true when you see animals), and most times it's confirmation that you're on the right path. Below are some of the ways your spirit team may try to communicate with you.

Messages From Your Spirit Team

- **Synchronicity:** Instead of viewing certain events in your life as a coincidence, synchronicity is knowing and understanding that these events are intentional and are serving your growth and healing. A Godincidence. It could be something you see in nature, an animal that crosses your path, a song that comes on the radio, a well-timed email or phone call, or even something that shows up on an Internet search. All of these are guidance from your spirit team.

- **Feelings:** This type of communication is about feeling the message or presence of your spirit team, God, the angels, or a departed loved one. At times it may be confusing deciphering if what you're feeling is guidance from your spirit team or if it's your own intuition. Essentially, they are both one and the same since spirit communicates through your intuition and gut feelings, so trust your feelings, knowing you're right.

- **Sounds:** Some people can physically hear messages from their spirit team, just as you hear other noises around you. It can be a little jolting, but the messages are powerful and for your highest good.

- **Visions:** Other people see visions from their spirit team, either physically with their eyes or with a vision showing up in their minds. An image or vision from your spirit team is a way for them to convey a message to you in a way you can understand and process it.

- **Numbers:** This type of communication from your spirit team is very common. Seeing repeating numbers like 11:11 and 1:11 or seeing a certain number sequence repeatedly means your spirit team is trying to get your attention to let you know they are here supporting you.

You get messages from your spirit team all the time but you are often busy and distracted so you might miss them. If you pay attention, divine support is all around you. Many times, your spirit team supports you using nature. It may be the wildlife you see out your window or the unexpected rain shower that comes at a time when you need an energetic rinsing. Other times it's the right person who comes into your life at the right time, to deliver the exact information you need.

Spirit can also influence your electronic devices, so your support will be the solution you need that has popped up on your Internet search. It's also the book you pick up, with the perfect message you need to see. Your angels love to send you messages through music too, such as a song you hear in the grocery store or in your car. Support from your angels will give you both clarity and insight. The messages you receive from your support team are positive and encouraging, guiding you to wholeness.

After my grandmother died, I started to receive messages of support from her through birds and flowers. I live on five acres surrounded by trees, so it's not uncommon to see birds around my house. However, my grandmother died in December, when most birds have already flown south for the winter. After she died, I regularly saw birds flying and perched outside my office window. I even had a bird tapping loudly on my sliding glass door just days after she died. In fact, as I'm writing this there are at least a dozen birds flying right outside my office window in January and in 17-degree temperatures (with the wind chill it's five degrees!). I believe this is my grandmother's way of giving me a wink as I'm writing this section. (Did I mention that our spirit team has a good sense of humor too?)

When my grandmother was alive, she frequently used to ask about my orchids. While I have been able to keep most of my orchids alive, I had never been able to get them to bloom again in the 10 years that I've had them. That is, until my grandmother died. One week after she died, I saw buds on one plant. The next week my other orchid had buds and within a few weeks my orchids were in full bloom. The orchids and birds are some of the ways my grandmother communicates with me.

Even difficult situations are guidance from your spirit team. Sometimes we have to get through some difficult situations in order to unlock the healing that needs to take place. Difficulties don't mean your spirit team has turned their back on you or that things aren't going in the right direction. Just know that many of the hard times you go through are for your growth and healing. Sometimes you have to go through the hardships to set your soul free.

EMOTIONAL AND PHYSICAL SUPPORT

Anxiety is an indicator that there is a significant lack of support in your life and cracks in your foundation. Inadequate support feels like you've been carrying around leaden weights that are holding you down and maybe even drowning you. You probably don't even realize you're carrying around dead weights because you've become accustomed to them. It's all you know.

Each of these dead weights dragging you down is an unsupportive person or situation, someone who expects you to be there for them but is not there for you. It may be people who expect you to live your life by their rules or people who don't truly see, hear, and know the real you. It may also be situations that drain you—your time, resources, and energy. If you want to heal anxiety, it is imperative that you have unwavering support in your life. You can't heal anxiety while carrying around dead weight. Your unsupportive relationships will only continue to hold you down until you are completely drained and have nothing left.

In the next section, you'll learn tools to free yourself from the dead weights that are holding you down so that you can free yourself from anxiety. I know it can feel scary to release all the toxic dysfunction around you when that's all you know. But once you do, you will be able to hear your own voice, maybe for the first time. You'll free up your time, energy, and resources to devote to your healing and inner growth. You deserve to be free.

ILLUSIONS

The first step to creating a solid foundation is the hardest part—seeing through illusions. There is nothing you actively need to do to see through the illusions in your life. When you are in a relationship with the divine and accepting their support and guidance, illusions will be shown to you through messages that are in sync with your soul growth and healing. Trust your messages.

With the steady support of your spirit team, layers of illusions will begin to lift so that you can see who is supporting you physically and emotionally. Your spirit team will show you one by one who unconditionally loves and supports you and, sadly, who doesn't. Your angels will help you see those in your life for who they really are rather than who you need them to be or who they are pretending to be. You'll learn to discern who is supportive of you and who is detracting from you and negatively impacting your mental health.

When you see through illusions, you may get clarity about someone who is in a position of authority and who is in fact abusing their power. Illusions lifting may also manifest by seeing a close friend whom you believed was genuine and kind behave maliciously and selfishly. Removing illusions can be accepting the truth about your parent or partner, that despite their title as "parent" or "partner," they are completely unsupportive of you. Seeing through illusions is "seeing" the truth no matter how hard and uncomfortable the truth is. The first few illusions may be hard to see but seeing the truth will get easier.

It's disappointing to see the truth that some family and friends are unsupportive and don't truly value you. Carrying unsupportive relationships, whether it's friends, family, coworkers, or business relationships, is a burden. It's extra weight that you need to let go of in order to heal yourself. Toxic and unsupportive relationships will only weigh you down. There's so much dysfunction in the world that you need to draw a line and not permit it in your inner circle. To heal anxiety, you need all of the love, support, encouragement, and positivity you can get.

Choosing to heal and live an authentic life will upset other people in your life for many reasons: they're not getting the attention they want, you're no longer allowing them to control your narrative, you're standing up for yourself, you're not excusing their inappropriate behavior, and a boat load of other reasons. Many of these people will drift away as you continue to nurture and heal yourself. Honestly, these people were never in your corner before you chose to heal. They probably never treated you with the love and respect that you deserve.

110 PERCENT

I used to give 110 percent of myself to my relationships—family, friends, professional, and business relationships. I prioritized everyone else's needs over my own. While trying to take care of everyone else in my life, I was neglecting myself. I never questioned this dynamic because it's all I knew. My relationships left me feeling emotionally starved and exhausted because my focus was consistently on everyone else. I recklessly assumed that since I was working so hard on my relationships, that these people were doing the same for me. I projected that these people had my best intentions in mind as I did for them. As a result, I was unaccustomed to identifying my own needs, much less fulfilling them.

You may also be programmed to habitually put other's needs before your own. But to heal anxiety, your soul desperately needs you to return to yourself. Most people with anxiety don't have a clue about how to receive in relationships. You may only know how to give to the point where you have nothing left. Instead, you must learn to redirect your focus, time, and energy back to yourself so that you can unearth your own needs and ensure they are met. In identifying and prioritizing your needs, you'll be more equipped to receive help and support from the relationships where you are seen, heard, and loved unconditionally. It's time for you to release the relationships that don't value you, or, at a minimum, limit your time with them.

Giving 110 percent, or even 100 percent, is not sustainable. If you're giving 90 percent, but only getting 10 percent in return, that 10 percent is not enough to sustain you. Your heart needs love to thrive. In toxic relationships you're only feeding your heart breadcrumbs when you need the whole loaf of bread to heal and flourish. Breadcrumbs may temporarily pacify your hunger for support without any real nourishment, leaving you ravenous for true support.

BREADCRUMBS

Breadcrumbs are the occasional bits of positivity you get from unhealthy relationships. Since you rarely get them, it's almost shocking when you do, and it feels so nice. It's like you've been walking in the desert, and then you finally get a sip of water after being completely dehydrated. But you only get one sip. While that sip of water may feel glorious in the moment, it's not enough to quench your thirst.

Similarly, in some of your relationships, you may be constantly criticized, but once in a blue moon they'll toss you a compliment. You may be entirely unseen in other relationships except for the once-a-year birthday shout-out they post on your social media page. In other toxic relationships you'll be both ignored and criticized until they want something from you and are kind to you for a day. These are examples of breadcrumbs. They keep you hooked but are not enough to sustain you. In fact, they completely drain you and can affect your health.

Everyone needs the whole loaf, especially if you're healing an illness like anxiety. If all you're getting is breadcrumbs, then you are slowly starving to death without realizing it. Even if you have great intentions, you cannot live your best life if you are surrounded by unsupportive people who feed you breadcrumbs. Not only are you slowly starving to death, but when your support crew consists mostly of unsupportive relationships, you begin to see the world through their lens. Because their narrative is so loud and distracting, it becomes your narrative. The dramas and diversions from these toxic relationships are affecting how you see yourself and the world around you– they cloud your vision so you cannot see the world and all the sunshine and bright colors it offers. The energy of these relationships inevitably rubs off on you, leaving you feeling stuck, drained, and confused.

When you realize you deserve the whole loaf and clear these relationships from your life, or at a minimum limit your interactions with them, your vision becomes clear. Over time you start to hear your own voice, instead of their voices, in your head. Many times, when you're engaged in dysfunctional relationships, their energy becomes enmeshed with your own. If you're an empath, you may be confused as to which are your feelings and which are theirs (I talked about this in chapter one). As you clear these unsupportive relationships from your life, you clean your own energy as the energy of others rinses out of you.

As you detach from dramas and distractions, your vision becomes very clear, so clear that you view your life with balance, openness, integrity, and most importantly, trust in yourself. With restored vision, you're able to handle the stresses in your life with confidence and clarity. You will know who and what's right for you. You will also be in a better place to discern who gets access into your life and who doesn't. There's no more settling because now you call the shots. You're putting an end to the stuck record playing in the background the repeating message of "you're not good enough."

Using your own lens, you become attuned and aligned to your own energy and your unique voice. You become astute about different people and situations that want admittance into your life. You trust your intuition if you have a weird feeling about someone or something. You also trust your gut when you meet someone who has good intentions. You are able to discern the relationships that are rooted in respect and integrity. The more you return to yourself, the more you are able to distinguish what feels right and what feels off.

NARCISSISM

Learning about narcissistic personalities provides a lot of clarity as to who is supportive in your life and who isn't. This type of behavior is often rampant in the relationships surrounding those who have anxiety. Relationships with narcissistic people often leave you feeling confused, devalued, unseen, and unheard. People with narcissistic behavior think nothing of taking from you in order to bolster themselves. They will take from you until you have nothing left and then move on to the next person. These kinds of toxic relationships are the source of your broken self-trust and the subsequent cause of your anxiety.

Narcissism is defined as a personality type that's extremely self-centered and causes people with it to lack empathy. In addition to selfishness, narcissists also feel extremely entitled. They use different techniques to try and control the people in their lives such as guilt, manipulation, and gaslighting (which I discussed in chapter one). The repercussions of maintaining these narcissistic relationships take a massive toll on your mental, spiritual, and physical health.

Dr. Ramani Durvasula is a psychologist who specializes in narcissist personalities. I highly recommend reading her book *Don't You Know Who I Am?* to educate yourself about narcissism. Dr. Christiane Northrup's book *Dodging Energy Vampires* is another great book to learn about narcissism and how to protect yourself and your energy from them, especially if you're an empath. Both books describe narcissists and both books note that narcissists will never change. The person who has to change is you, by becoming adept at spotting their behavior and steering clear of them.

I'm not sure if narcissism has increased recently or if now that there's a name for this behavior it's easier to identify. Regardless, these relationships take a toll on you. Ideally, it's best to avoid narcissistic relationships and at a minimum limit your interaction with narcissists with fierce boundaries intact.

Dr. Durvasula describes 30 traits of narcissism in her book but lists the following seven as the main traits that constitute the core of narcissism. If someone you know exhibits one, two, or just a few of the 30 traits, then that person is most likely is just rude (not great!) but not necessarily a narcissist. However, someone who displays most or all of the seven traits below is most likely a narcissist.

Seven Main Narcissist Traits

1. *Grandiosity* - This trait shows when the narcissist regularly talks themselves up, trying to make themselves appear more important, accomplished, and popular than they really are. They'll proclaim that they're the greatest, the most involved, best liked, and/or most talented.

2. *Entitlement* - A narcissistic person habitually shows entitlement, believing that they deserve special treatment. They behave as if it is below them to have to do every day, normal things. Some examples include, but are not limited to, impatience about waiting in lines, demanding exclusive treatment, or never arriving on time to social engagements.

3. *Lack of Empathy* - An individual with this trait rarely, if ever, cares about the feelings of others. They are poor listeners, uncompassionate, and often dismiss the needs and feelings of others.

4. *Validation Seeking* - A narcissistic individual needs a constant supply of validation all day and every day. It's their lifeline. Validation seekers continually make everything about themselves. They'll frequently shift conversations so as to talk about themselves endlessly. Their need for external validation is like an addiction.

5. *Superficiality* - This refers to the narcissist's obsession with external appearances. It might be the clothes they wear, the car they drive, cosmetic surgery, an immaculate house, and/or over-the-top vacations. These people invest a lot of time

and resources to look perfect, when underneath this layer of superficiality everything is a mess.

6. *Hypersensitivity to Criticism* - Narcissists cause you to feel hypervigilant when you deal with them because they get upset at the slightest perceived infraction. They live in a fantasy world where they believe they are perfect and the slightest criticism, whether intentional or unintentional, will set them off.

7. *Emotional Dysregulation* - Since narcissistic people are completely out of touch with their emotions, they become emotionally dysregulated. Instead of building their self-esteem intrinsically, they rely on external validations. Because they are so insecure and emotionally dysregulated, they exhibit rage when they are dealing with difficult emotions. It will feel like you're walking on eggshells with this individual.

After looking at this list, you might be wondering if you're a narcissist because you at times exhibit some of these traits. The truth is everyone exhibits narcissistic traits sometimes. You're not perfect (thank goodness!), but that doesn't mean you're a narcissist. For a narcissist, this behavior becomes pathological, meaning they repeatedly exhibit these behaviors. Additionally, a narcissist doesn't have the capacity to reflect on their own behavior at all. If you're reading this and questioning if you're a narcissist, you're not. A narcissist will rarely own up to their mistakes.

Recently, I was thinking about what movie I wanted to watch while I ran on the treadmill. The movie *There's Something About Mary* popped into my head, which I hadn't thought about for more than 20 years. The movie kept coming to mind, so I knew it was a message from my spirit team, and I eventually decided to watch it. Watching the romantic comedy again, I had some big revelations. The movie felt like my life! Mary, played by Cameron Diaz, is a kind, compassionate, and successful woman. Throughout the movie, we see all of these guys who are romantically interested in Mary. Most of the guys are pretending to be kind and compassionate like Mary. The guys modify their behavior and sometimes their appearance to get Mary's attention and admiration.

At the end of the movie, Ted, who's played by Ben Stiller, calls out all of the other guys who are lying to Mary about who they really are. He says, "None of them love you, really. They're just fixated on you because of how you make them feel about themselves. That's not real love. I don't know what that is." I know what that is—narcissism! What Ted says to Mary is spot on about all of the other phony guys. It isn't love and, sadly, that's how it is in narcissistic relationships. Their interactions with you have nothing to do with you. It's all about how you make the narcissist feel about themselves. It's really sick and disturbing.

Throughout the movie, Mary accepts these phony guys for who they say they are, with no questions. Sure, she seems to have some inhibitions, but she ignores her gut and believes the guys. Then, with the help of Ben Stiller's character, Mary sees the men for who they really are—creepy self-centered guys who want to ride the coattails of her upbeat energy. By the end of the movie, veils are lifted, and illusions are revealed to show Mary who is real and authentic in her life, who is truly supportive of her, who is part of her support network, and who will weaken it.

I used to think that most of my relationships were good. Once I learned about narcissists, I discovered that I was surrounded by them, like Mary. They were family members, friends, and even business relationships. The experience was like peeling an onion. I first saw the narcissists who weren't that close to me. Then, as I started to evaluate my relationships and began peeling back the layers of the onion, I saw that toxic people were closer to me than I realized. These people really didn't care about me. Seeing the truth about who I was allowing in my inner circle was a huge step in healing my anxiety. The truth allowed me to take steps to protect my energy, to feel safe, and to trust myself again knowing that all my hunches had been right.

It's hard to see and accept that your family and friends don't love and accept you unconditionally. It's hard to see that they don't have your best interest at heart and probably never will. The hardest part to see is that they will never change. The only one who will change is you, and you have to change your expectations.

As veils are lifted and you start to see the truth behind the illusions, you may also see that you're surrounded by dysfunction. For many of you, this dysfunction is all you've ever known. Honestly acknowledging your relationships for what they are is the hardest step. It's heartbreaking to know that not everything is as it seems, and it can feel like your world is crumbling apart. Not everyone has kind intentions and that's extremely painful to witness. It can feel like the Twilight Zone. The people you thought were genuine instead have ulterior, self-serving motives. When you've always been surrounded by these people it gets confusing because dysfunction has been your norm. Since it's all you've ever known, you may not realize there's another way.

With anxiety, you have to acknowledge the truth if you want to heal. Anxiety arises when you are not honest and authentic with yourself. Just like I discussed in chapter one about your feelings and emotions, if you do not honestly acknowledge your emotions and allow them to move through you in a way that feels authentic, this creates anxiety in your body. Anything that does not align with integrity will activate anxiety. Along this line of thinking, if you are not honest about who is supportive of you, anxiety will surface.

Your body knows the truth. Your souls know the truth. You can't fool yourself and when you try to, it will only hurt you and hold you back from bravely stepping forward as your true self. Sometimes your true self is scared and that's normal, as long as you take an honest look around, honor the truth, and move forward in integrity.

Identifying narcissistic relationships in your life is complicated and confusing. That's where your spirit team comes in. Since relationships with narcissists wreak havoc on you physically, emotionally, and spiritually, you need your spirit team to lead the way. Your spirit team will gently highlight the narcissists in your life for you. They will give you clues, signs, and messages about all of the dysfunction and toxicity in your life. They will speak to you through your intuition to show you the truth. Signs you may have missed before will now become obvious. You'll be able to read between the lines of what a narcissist is really saying and doing. Your spirit team wants you to be fully supported here on earth.

FALL SEASON

When the fog begins to lift and you can see who is true and supportive in your life, it's time to be selective about who you surround yourself with. As the seasons transition from summer into fall, trees adapt for survival during the coming colder months. In the fall, trees drop their leaves to prepare for winter. In the winter, the leaves are no longer needed so they are shed in order for trees to conserve their resources and hunker down to survive the cold winters.

Any relationship that is not supporting you is jeopardizing your survival. Just as trees transition in the fall, you must shed all that isn't supporting you so that you can focus on your healing. You need to focus your time and energy on yourself and healing anxiety, rather than on unhealthy relationships that thrive on drama. You can't support your own healing while constantly being distracted by others or by overextending yourself. And there's a good chance that your anxiety either stemmed from and/or is perpetuated by these toxic relationships.

RELEASING TOXIC PEOPLE

Sadly, not everyone wants to see you succeed. There are probably people in your life who don't want to see you do well. They may be friends, family, coworkers, or really anyone. The people who criticize you for having anxiety will also judge you for making time and space to heal. They might even ridicule you for prioritizing your healing. These people are cruel and uncompassionate. They are not part of your support team, and they need to be released. When you release your unhealthy relationships, you inadvertently make space for healthy relationships.

Fear of change and fear of being alone causes people to stay in relationships that are way past their prime. The fear of the unknown, the fear of something new, or the fear that there aren't better options paralyze many people into staying in dysfunctional relationships. These are all legitimate concerns, but the worst-case scenario, being alone, is better than being treated poorly. When you're healing, nothing less than true support will do.

Toxic relationships leave you feeling drained and isolated. They make you feel less than, wasting time and your precious energy. You're in a constant state of stress because you're perpetually walking on eggshells, which results in anxiety. You need relief from these relationships so your endocrine and nervous systems can stabilize and strengthen. It's time to end these relationships, or at a minimum, limit your time with them.

RELEASING TOXIC PLACES AND SITUATIONS

What places or situations make you feel uncomfortable? Creating unwavering support also requires you to evaluate where you spend time, physically or virtually. Start observing how you feel in different situations. Are there certain places that make you feel more anxious? Know that it's OK if there are places or situations that don't work for you. All places and environments are not meant for everyone. It's up to you to figure out what works for you and what doesn't as you move along your healing journey. Spend time in those places and situations that fulfill you so that you can heal.

For some people, being in large crowds makes their skin crawl. They prefer a smaller, more intimate get-together compared to large gatherings. Other people crave large cities and thrive on the energy there. Virtual settings can cause angst in your body too, especially ones that thrive on drama. News outlets and social media feed on drama and can drain your energy and cause unnecessary stress.

Create boundaries about where you spend time to encourage your healing and growth. The environments and situations you spend time in will either deter your healing or fuel it. If you have to spend time in harsh places, make a deliberate effort to counterbalance it with protection practices (chapter one) and regular self-care (chapter four).

RELEASING TOXIC BUSINESS RELATIONSHIPS

Toxic relationships extend to business relationships too. When you pay money for a product or service, you expect a good product and service. If the person on the other end of the business relationship is not living up to their end of the agreement, it's time to move on. If the person you're in a business relationship with is not treating you with kindness and respect, it's time to bail. Business arrangements are not charity. You choose where you spend your money. Too many times people stay in dysfunctional business relationships out of fear of change and not knowing what other options are out there.

If your doctor isn't listening to your concerns or taking you seriously, find another doctor who will. If your favorite restaurant begins to rush you through your meal to bring more people in, try some new restaurants. If your yoga teacher is habitually late or overly critical, find another school or learning platform to take a class. Do your research and see what other options there are. You should never feel tied down in any relationship, including business relationships. Your business relationships should support you too—you're paying for it!

Below are some questions to help you identify the relationships you need to release or limit.

Discerning Relationships You Need to Release

1. How do you feel most of the time in this relationship?
2. Does this relationship make you constantly doubt yourself?
3. Do you feel safe showing your true self in this relationship?
4. Are you supported for your successes as well as your losses?
5. Is this relationship meeting your needs?
6. Do you feel seen and heard in this relationship?

Benefit of the Doubt

When determining the relationships that are worth nurturing, you might fall into a pattern of giving someone the benefit of the doubt. According to Dr. Ramani, psychologist, author, and expert in the field of narcissism, the benefit of the doubt constitutes enabling.

Our culture highly encourages giving people the benefit of the doubt, declaring it an act of kindness. Sometimes there are cases where giving someone the benefit of the doubt is reasonable. However, if you're consistently giving someone the benefit of the doubt, you're effectually excusing their rude or hurtful behavior.

There's another component too. When you continually give someone the benefit of the doubt or make excuses for someone, you're not trusting your intuition. If someone says or does something to cause you to doubt them, that's your intuition stepping in. On subtler levels, your intuition is picking up on clues about this person's character and integrity. When you intuitively know that something isn't right, you should listen to your gut. Kindness isn't second guessing your intuition. Kindness is heeding the information your intuition gives you for your protection.

Your gut feelings and intuition are also how spirit communicates with you and if your gut feels off, your spirit team is giving you a clear message about that individual. Your spirit team will make it clear when relationships or situations are not supporting you. You'll see or hear things you normally wouldn't have. Phone calls may get repeatedly cut off or emails will get garbled. Trust that your spirit team is communicating with you about who's supporting you. Know they will also put people in your path who will fully support you.

"YOU'RE EITHER WITH ME OR GET THE HECK OUT OF MY WAY"

As I was building my support network, I created a slogan that helped me identify who was supportive: You're either with me or get the heck out of my way! (Except, I didn't use the word heck!) The gist of this slogan is that I'm moving forward on my path, whether or not you like it. You can choose to support me or step aside because I will never again allow anyone to hold me back.

This slogan helped me to build the resiliency I needed to follow through on some of my dreams, including writing this book. As I started my journey to healing and writing, I quickly learned who was in my corner and who didn't want to see me succeed. When I was starting to build my self-trust, this slogan was a reminder for me to stay focused on myself and ignore the voices and opinions of others. And I'm so glad I did! Hopefully, this slogan will serve as a reminder for you too. If not, create your own, as long as it's something that keeps you focused when the people around you are doubting you or trying to hold you back.

GRIEF

If you're ending a toxic relationship, you will most likely feel relief at first—relief from the stress, drama, and, in some cases, abuse. However, it is normal to also grieve the loss of these relationships even though they were toxic. What you're actually grieving is the loss of your expectations of the relationship and/or person. You're sad about what that person could have been in your life or how the relationship could have been. You're not really sad for losing how it actually was. For example, if you have ended contact with a toxic parent, your grief may be about what it would have been like if your parent supported you and loved you unconditionally. You might be grieving that you'll never have that kind of relationship with your parent. Your grief is completely normal.

If doubts creep in (which is normal too), remember the relief you felt when you ended the relationship. Remember that relief and hold onto to it. That relief came from being free of the pain and negativity inherent in that relationship. It's your body telling you that you've escaped a dangerous situation.

> *"And so rock bottom became the solid foundation on which I rebuilt my life."*
>
> — *J.K. ROWLING*

This quote from J.K. Rowling resonates with the time in my life when I realized that the people I considered friends and family did not have my best interest at heart. I make it a priority to live my life out of integrity. I don't always get it right, but I always do my best. My mistake was assuming everyone else was doing the same.

For me, hitting rock bottom was finding myself alone after releasing these dysfunctional relationships. I wasn't really alone though—I had my spiritual support and my husband and kids. I just felt alone. I took my feeling of aloneness and built a beautiful support network where my needs are heard and met, and my soul's growth is supported.

Releasing all the people who are unsupportive of you isn't easy. In the process of shedding your leaves you discover who is part of your support network. Releasing all of the dysfunction frees up a lot of your time and energy. Use this time to build a solid spiritual practice to strengthen your connection with the divine and to learn about your needs and ensure they are met. Spend more time getting to know yourself and hear your soul like you never have before.

TRUE SUPPORT

True support is gracious and understanding. At times, one person in a respectful and supportive relationship may be doing more of the supportive work while the other is going through a difficult time. But when the tables are turned, the person who received does the helping. Spending time with supportive people will fill you up, instead of draining you. You'll feel built up instead of torn down. Furthermore, supportive relationships will reinforce your self-trust instead of leaving you constantly questioning yourself. Some relationships are so supportive that you may find yourself becoming fully comfortable sharing your soul.

When you have anxiety, you most likely have no clue about what true support looks like or feels like. There's a dance that takes place in true supportive relationships and this dance isn't always in tandem. Instead of thinking of the dynamics of supportive relationships in terms of give and take, I prefer to use the words share and receive.

Your primary responsibility is to take care of yourself. You've heard the analogy of putting on your oxygen mask first before helping someone else. The same concept applies to your relationships. You can't give what you don't have or don't have enough of. Giving to the point where you have nothing left is unsustainable. Giving also suggests you're giving something of yourself, whereas sharing means you have enough for yourself too. You can only share with others as long as it doesn't detract from yourself.

You also have to get used to receiving in relationships too. As I mentioned with anxiety, you may be used to giving of yourself until you're completely depleted and exhausted, so it may take time to get used to finally receiving the support you desperately need and deserve. It's time to allow yourself to receive love and support and to be seen, heard, and cherished, to be on the receiving end of what others have to share with you.

Most importantly, supportive relationships are never about taking. Taking suggests someone is grabbing something that isn't theirs or that they don't have your permission to take it. Taking is also very aggressive—the exact opposite of what you need to heal. Put the brakes on any relationship that feels like it's taking from you as soon as possible. You cannot heal while constantly giving of yourself. Unsupportive relationships rarely share and mostly take, which is completely different from receiving.

YOUR SUPPORT CREW

A small support crew that is solid and unwavering is better for your overall health than a large group of people who don't support you. As I mentioned earlier, unsupportive people can be friends, family members, or coworkers who expect you to show them steadfast support while continually disappearing when you need support. Some will make a show of being supportive, but if you look closely, it's really not support and it's all about them, while others simply prefer to see you not do well. All of these types of unsupportive people are toxic and take a toll on your health and mental wellbeing, while continuing to rob you of your time, energy, and resources until you have nothing left.

One by one you can selectively start piecing together your support crew. This crew will be your cheering squad who are rallying for you and who believe in you. Your support crew may be smaller than you originally thought, but it will be more solid. It's the quality, not the size, of your support that counts. Fewer support columns that are made of steel are more supportive than many columns made of foam. Nurturing and emotionally investing in the relationships that are supportive is better for your health, including your mental health.

Everyone needs at least one person in their corner rooting for them. When you're dealing with anxiety, it can feel like you're in the ocean getting pummeled by waves, one after another. All it takes is just one person to offer you their hand to pull you out of the surf so that you can stand on your own two feet again, someone who will actually listen to you and accept you as you are—not for how they can change you or for what you can do for them, one person who believes in your dreams and encourages you to follow them.

This person can be a friend, family member, spouse, coach, or therapist, someone who truly sees you and all of your greatness, someone who respects and validates you.

Just like a house plant that receives plenty of sunshine and adequate water and nutrients grows and thrives, you too will grow, thrive, and heal when you are nurtured. You deserve this kind of support.

The ultimate goal for any relationship you choose to engage in is relationship harmony. Relationship harmony exists when there is open honest communication about your feelings and emotions as well as your needs and wants. It goes both ways, with both parties communicating openly and honestly. Relationship harmony requires both people to invest their time and effort into the relationship after they've invested in themselves.

YOUR COCOON

As you're healing and rebuilding your foundation and support network it's normal to form a cocoon around yourself. Your cocoon is where the process of metamorphosis takes place. You need a safe and cozy place where you can fall apart and put yourself back together again. Your cocoon can be your home, a separate room, closet, or even just a corner in a room. Fill this space with everything you love, things that bring you joy —art, crafts, music, crystals, cards, whatever moves your soul. Ideally, this should be a space where you can get some quiet time to sort out your thoughts and feelings as you heal. This space should feel comforting and nurturing to you because this is where you will spend the bulk of your time healing.

Your cocoon is similar to a cocoon that transforms a caterpillar into a butterfly. Safely tucked in your cocoon, you will shed layers of your old self that you no longer need. Shedding these layers will make you feel exposed and emotionally naked. You're peeling off layers of dysfunction so that you can hear your own voice and nurture your soul. You will feel like you've turned to mush, but this stage is only temporary even though it feels like it will last forever.

Your cocoon is where you will uncover your soul. As you continue to care for and nurture yourself and build your self-trust, you will eventually feel safe and strong enough to emerge from your cocoon and share your beauty with the world. With all those layers shed, your internal light will shine so brightly that you'll be a beacon of light for others who are ready to go through their own metamorphosis too.

Take as long as you need in your cocoon, your physical and emotional isolation. Seeing through layers upon layers of illusions and dysfunction, you may feel unsure who to trust outside of your spirit team. In the safety of your cocoon, you will rebuild and strengthen your foundation and create unwavering support. You will address everything that you've been keeping in the dark and which needs healing. After facing your fears and some dark nights of the soul, you will come out into the light transformed. Your darkness is not necessarily bad. It's the parts of you that need love and attention.

While nurturing supportive relationships are important, you also will get to know yourself better and become comfortable spending time by yourself. Even though this may seem terrifying to some people, it's important to heal anxiety. When you are comfortable being alone or mostly alone, then you're not welcoming people in your life to fill a void. Being content on your own means there is no void.

Time spent hearing your own voice, implementing self-care, and nurturing your needs, wants, and dreams creates your new standard for relationships. If you already enjoy spending time on your own and are feeding your soul good quality nourishment, there's no need or room in your life for toxic and dysfunctional relationships or situations that will only bring you down. And something interesting happens too. As you drop the dysfunctional relationships and care for yourself, you create room for supportive relationships. Your relationships from here on out must give you the whole loaf and nothing less.

I had a lifelong destructive pattern of people pleasing that I brought into my cocoon. While it served others well, it was destroying me as my voice was getting drowned out by the needs of others. On my journey to boldly trusting myself, I had to drop the unsupportive and toxic relationships around me while I was in my cocoon. In my cocoon, the darkness I faced was the fear of being alone. I had to face the fear that in doing what was right for me and my family, I would upset others. I had to let go of trying to control the feelings of others. I spent a couple of years in my cocoon finally hearing myself and emerged knowing my worth. I stopped putting the thoughts and feelings of other people before my own. As a butterfly, stepping into my light, I now invest in me. I do things that light me up. I only do things when it's a definite yes. And I've learned how to say no.

This time spent in your cocoon can feel very uncomfortable but treasure this time. It is pivotal for your healing. This is where the magic happens. This time alone is needed to help you to step back and observe where the dysfunction was. Listen deeply for what your soul has to say, because your soul is getting ready to take flight. Trusting your spirit team and piecing together unwavering support establishes the framework for you to trust your own light and start shining.

4

I TRUST MY LIGHT

"Luminous beings are we, not this crude matter."

— YODA, *STAR WARS EPISODE V: THE
EMPIRE STRIKES BACK*

YOU HAVE A UNIQUE, BRILLIANT LIGHT THAT DESERVES TO shine brightly. Your beautiful light is desperately needed and is part of God's divine plan. When you shine your light, you also encourage others to do the same because as you authentically express your soul, others feel safe to follow suit. As everyone shines their respective lights, the entire planet will light up and will outshine all of the darkness.

Shining your light means authentically expressing yourself. It's boldly living your life on your terms at the risk of walking alone. It's doing what you believe is right in your heart even when it's different from what others believe. It's knowing you deserve love and respect and that you will never again settle for anything less. It's embracing your inherent strength and power, knowing it will probably make others uncomfortable. It's loving and honoring every aspect of yourself and investing in your self-care.

You cannot heal anxiety while simultaneously hiding your light. Hiding your light creates and feeds anxiety. Trying to keep your light contained and muted only hurts you. I use the word "trying" because your soul can never be contained or dimmed, but the act of trying to mute your light spawns anxiety.

After living with debilitating anxiety for 20 years and healing it, I've come up with my own definition of anxiety based on my observations and experiences:

Anxiety is the unconscious and continual gaslighting of yourself while making yourself small to accommodate others.

I believe people with anxiety unknowingly gaslight themselves in order to dim their lights. In this chapter I'll further unravel gaslighting to uncover the reasons why people do so. I'll also share why hiding your light creates anxiety so that you can finally heal and safely shine your light.

HIDING YOUR LIGHT

Someone who is hiding their light is living in a box with a set of limitations that they've bought into. People do it all the time, and I did too. Many people adopt personal beliefs that unknowingly dampen their light. These people both consciously and unconsciously make themselves small. They are not living to their fullest potential because they believe they are not enough, and so they limit themselves. People are indoctrinated into beliefs that label, stratify, and constrain them and others for their differences instead of honoring and nurturing them.

Remember my definition of anxiety? I'm going to delve into the second part of my definition—"making ourselves small to accommodate others." Some people are severely threatened by your light, and you dim your light so that these people feel less intimidated by you. You dim it to feel accepted and to fit in. These people live in self-imposed boxes and limit themselves. Even worse, they want you to limit yourself and make yourself small.

Living your life fully and unbounded while blazing past their limitations sets these people off. You are a reminder to them of what they are choosing not to be. You threaten them because they need you to be small so that they can feel better about themselves and their choices.

"If you fight for your limitations, you get to keep them."

— JIM KWIK, *LIMITLESS*

If someone is threatened by your light and your success, they are not meant for you. If others are adamant about their prescribed set of self-imposed limits, then by all means they can limit themselves and live in their box, as the quote above highlights. It's not your job to live in their box to appease them.

These same people who limit themselves want to label and pigeonhole you. This makes them feel safe because they know where you stand. They want to ensure that you don't move past them and become more successful by whatever their definition of success is. Be wary of labels and those who use them—they are dangerous. If you adhere to them too much, they limit you and start to define your behavior. Labels can be a prison for your soul.

Most likely in the past you were punished or shunned for shining your light. Maybe a parent shut you down when you started to express your natural talents or gifts. A friend may have mocked or criticized you as you were taking action steps to follow through on your dreams. A coworker may have downplayed your contributions to a project.

Most people who dim their lights do it out of conditioned fear from past punishment and pain. They then associate their light with shame, hurt, and embarrassment. They're justly concerned others won't like them and will shun them if they stop hiding and express themselves authentically.

Observing and acknowledging where you are limiting yourself will give you clarity about where you need love, tenderness, and support. Exposing the areas of your life where you are dimming your light allows you to gently step out of your box to give yourself freedom to live your life on your terms and to heal anxiety. Healing anxiety is all about freeing yourself from the chains that are trying to hold you down, including invalidation and shame.

INVALIDATION

Invalidation is a prevalent and insidious technique employed by narcissists. When you are invalidated, the abuser downplays your experiences or flat out denies them. With a narcissist, you and your experiences aren't given any airtime. The narcissist may pretend that certain events in your life never happened or will try to convince you that it played out differently than you vividly remember.

Invalidation is a deliberate manipulation tactic used by the narcissist to destabilize trust in yourself so that they can wedge themselves into a position of trust in your life. Over time you mistakenly shift trust from yourself to the narcissist, which they in turn use to manipulate and control you. They want to control you so that you constantly feed their fragile egos. They need you to make them feel good about themselves. Fueling their egos, termed "narcissistic supply," is the narcissist's lifeline. They cannot survive without it. They essentially try to break you down to ensure you stick around to inflate them.

Invalidating you and your experiences in addition to deeply entrenched patterns of gaslighting shatters your self-trust. Your version of reality is fed to you by the "reality" the narcissist feeds you. Invalidation and gaslighting is intended to confuse you, disrupting trust in your intuition and your own feelings. It shatters your self-worth and sets the stage for a lifetime of people pleasing. You begin to place your self-worth and emotional well-being into the hands of others, specifically narcissists.

I have had family members who would not acknowledge my huge accomplishments in addition to the smaller events in my life: my education, running a marathon, and even the birth of my children. This was extremely confusing! I worked hard to gain the approval of these family members only to be continually invalidated. Eventually, I also began to downplay my own successes and feared the spotlight for fear of their criticisms. In addition to never feeling good enough, I also felt personally responsible whenever something went wrong. I was dimming my light.

People who are in a relationship with a narcissist are usually not fully present in themselves due to all of the gaslighting and invalidation they've received. They are so focused on anticipating the needs of the narcissist that they completely lose sight of their own needs and stop hearing their own voice. They don't know their worth and never feel like they're enough. They are desperate for external validation because of all of the breadcrumbs (see chapter three) they've received. Sadly, in narcissistic relationships, that validation will never come. It has to come from inside yourself.

Know that when someone invalidates you, it's more about them than it ever is about you. Their insecurities are controlling them. They're also giving you clues as to how they feel about themselves as they project their insecurities onto you. Just because a narcissist has emotional wounds and is acting out of insecurity is no excuse for invalidating, gaslighting, and emotionally abusing you. While their behavior is not personal, it's still unacceptable. Abuse is abuse regardless of the cause and needs to end. Your health depends on it!

Ending or limiting your relationships with narcissists allows you to know yourself and your own reality. As you become familiar with our own narrative, you start to see the whole picture clearly. As I discussed in chapter three, even though the truth can be painful, it will enable you to set your own narrative, boldly trust yourself, and free yourself from anxiety. The truth really does set you free. By bravely narrating your own life, you will discover your self-worth. You'll feel free and empowered when you discover that the only validation you need is your own.

Acknowledge where you've been invalidated so that you can begin to give yourself the validation you never received. Give yourself the unconditional love and acceptance you've always wanted. Treat yourself with the respect, kindness, and compassion you deserve. As you begin to embrace your worth, new people and experiences in your life will match your new feelings and celebrate you, honor you, and support your growth. I can't express enough how much peace is attained when you stop trusting toxic people. As you value your own thoughts and feelings over the opinion of others, you'll free yourself emotionally, shine your light freely, and free yourself from anxiety.

RELEASING SHAME

In addition to the destabilizing effects of being invalidated and gaslighted in toxic relationships, having anxiety itself has probably brought up strong and prolonged feelings of shame. You may have shame for having anxiety, for not being able to control it, for needing help, and for not being "normal." It's no wonder that the mental health stigma and the shame associated with anxiety makes you want to crawl under a giant rock and hide your light.

People with mental health conditions are not treated with the same level of compassion compared to others with more visible health problems. People who don't have anxiety or any other mental health conditions wrongly assume that anxiety is all in your head and therefore you can just make it stop, like flipping a light switch.

People who are insensitive and believe this think nothing of shaming and judging you for having anxiety. They assume you're choosing to have anxiety when the truth is people with anxiety would never wish anxiety on their worst enemy much less "choose" to have anxiety themselves. The cruel and insensitive judgments from others eventually interfere with your internal dialog. You feel shame because you can't turn your anxiety off. You think there is something wrong with you because you have anxiety. This shame paralyzes you into a deeply embedded belief that you're not good enough.

Author and researcher Brené Brown defines shame in her article "Shame vs. Guilt" as "the intensely painful feeling or experience of believing we're flawed and therefore unworthy of acceptance and belonging." Her research shows that the emotional pain you feel as the result of shame is cataloged by your brain as the same as physical pain, further demonstrating how destructive shame and the mental health stigma are. Unlike most physical pain, which eventually abates, the pain you feel with the anxiety stigma lingers, further perpetuating anxiety. This real continual pain detrimentally affects you physically, emotionally, and spiritually. The pain from shame further adds to the stress and adrenaline that created anxiety in the first place. It's no wonder that people with anxiety want to hide. The pain and discomfort from the shame and stigma are unbearable. Hiding your light may feel like the safest option, but it's not the answer. Hiding your light only hurts you.

NO MORE "SORRY"

How many times a day do you say "sorry?" Do you say sorry when you bump into someone accidentally? When you reach for something at the same time as someone else at a store? If you've missed your friend's text or phone call, do you apologize? Do you say sorry when you say "no" to someone? If you've answered yes to any of these questions, this section is for you. Always apologizing is an indicator that you are carrying around some level of shame and don't know your worth.

A proper apology when you've done something wrong is not what I'm talking about here. When I say no more "sorry," I'm talking about no more apologizing for your existence. If you're constantly saying sorry, most likely you've been gaslighted and invalidated into believing you're always in the wrong. If this has happened to you then "sorry" has unconsciously become part of your daily vernacular.

Saying sorry all of the time is another way of making yourself small to appease others. When I was dimming my light and making myself small, I apologized for everything. It was a combination of not being centered in myself, being an empath, and not knowing my worth as a result of the culmination of invalidation and gaslighting in my life.

You are not here by mistake. You are meant to be here at this time and are a part God's divine plan. There is a time and place for an apology, but not for everyday occurrences. Next time you accidentally step in front of someone or bump into them, an "excuse me" or "oops" will do. Hold your head up high and know that you are a gift to this world.

YOUR FOUNDATION

Your foundation is your self-worth and knowing you're enough, both of which create self-love. I mentioned in chapter three that you need a solid foundation to support your healing and soul growth. A strong foundation gives you solid footing to securely ground your light and feel safe shining it.

Building a solid foundation is an internal job and requires a lot of deep reflection and at times difficult choices. However, a strong foundation ensures that you will never be thrown off course again. You will only move in the direction of your true north, honoring your soul. Embracing your worth and loving yourself is foundational for healing as well as living.

You cannot effectively heal anxiety unless your foundation is rock solid. An unstable foundation is an easy breeding ground for anxiety. At the start of your healing journey, you may start to see that your foundation has massive cracks and is crumbling. This insight into your unsteady foundation is actually good because now you can start implementing changes to rebuild it. Once you reset your foundation, it will cure and become stronger as you travel your own unique path.

YOU ARE ENOUGH

Do you value yourself when you get a lot of work done during the day? Does checking everything off your "to do" list make you feel worthwhile? Do you feel guilty when you rest or have some down time? Answering "yes" to these questions highlights a deep-seated mindset of not feeling like you're enough. Feeling less than and never feeling like you're good enough is another reason you're dimming your light. The truth is you're enough just by simply being you, regardless of what you do or don't do.

Judging your "enoughness" based on what you do and how much you accomplish is a deeply ingrained belief that is harmful for both your physical and emotional health. Our culture bombards you with messages that your value is determined by what you do and how much you achieve. Society places so much value on your outputs instead of equally prioritizing your inputs. Your nourishment, rest, and restoration are ignored and get cast aside. You must refuel yourself emotionally, physically, and spiritually for your overall health and mental health. Constantly doing, pushing, and at times forcing is exhausting and will eventually wear you out.

It is admirable to have dreams and to take steps to achieve them. And there are times when you'll be working your butt off to accomplish them. However, rest and restoration must be part of the equation too. Just as there's a time to work hard, there also needs to be time allocated to recuperate and refill your energy reserves.

Most of your overall time is spent working towards your goals. Comparably, very little time is spent in the moment once you achieve your goal before moving onto the next project. Therefore, if you're spending most of your life working towards a goal, restoration and self-care needs to be a priority in order to live a sustainable and balanced life. Embracing a more sustainable work approach ensures your health and mental health are intact.

It's time to rewrite your narrative so that rest and restoration are a priority or at least have equal footing with your goals. Instead of basing your worth on how much you accomplish in a given day, week, or year, take pride in what you do to fill your heart and restore your soul. Take measures to bring passion and joy back into your life. Prioritize your down time just as much as your work time. Time spent resting and rejuvenating your heart, mind, and soul feeds creativity and nurtures inspiration. The interesting thing is that investing in self-care and restoration will, over time, make you more productive because your tank is full.

Restoration and self-care are important parts of investing in yourself and helping you move towards your goals. Prioritizing your self-care gives you pause to reflect on yourself and your work, allowing you to determine whether to continue in the same direction or pivot onto a path that's a better fit for you. Resting and taking breaks ensures you invest the best version of yourself into your project. You may be able to produce more by pushing yourself, but if you take care of yourself and work sustainably, you'll create better quality work.

It's good to have goals and to work diligently to accomplish them, but your goals don't define you. Accomplishments don't equal "enoughness." Always working and striving for the next big goal is unsustainable and will wear you out, negatively affecting your health and mental health. You don't have to do anything to prove your worth. Just you being you is enough, every day.

The unconscious belief that you are not enough plagues so many people, with and without mental health issues. This harmful mindset detrimentally impacts your mental

health, physical health, and soul growth. For most people
this message was instilled in you as a child, from those
you trusted and looked up to—parents, caregivers,
teachers, religious leaders, and maybe even doctors.
However, this message is also prevalent in our society with
advertising campaigns manipulating you to believe that
you're not good enough until you reach a certain weight
or drive an expensive car. There's money to be made by
keeping you small and feeling less than. Sadly, when you
don't believe you're enough, you hide your light.

MARY IN FULL COLOR

Never feeling good enough was ingrained in me as a child.
I was never encouraged to prioritize my own needs and
instead became adept at anticipating everyone else's
needs. Once I was married and had my own family, I
easily slipped into a pattern of prioritizing their needs
over my own and essentially lost myself in my family. I
even prioritized our extended family's and friends' needs
over my own. After what felt like a lifetime of people
pleasing and putting myself on the back burner, I was
completely drained. I was filling everyone else's tank
while gradually allowing my own tank to go empty. I
failed to put on my own oxygen mask first. Unable to
identify my own needs, much less communicate them, my
anxiety continued to worsen.

One of the first investments I made for myself on my
journey to heal anxiety was to join Kyle Gray's Angel
Team. Angel Team studied a different angel or spiritual

figure each month. My first year in Angel Team we studied Mother Mary during the month of May. During my guided meditation to connect with Mary, I saw Mary and Jesus standing in front of me! Mary was a dark silhouette standing slightly behind Jesus who was in full color. I was unsure about what my message was from Mary and frequently thought about what I saw for days after my meditation. Even though Mary was a dark silhouette, her energy was not dark or intimidating. In fact, she always feels strong, loving, protective, and steadfast to me—like a mama bear.

Meanwhile, during the rest of May, as I continued to study and work with Mary, I turned a corner in my healing. I began to see that I was hiding behind my family and not taking center stage in my own life because I never felt good enough and didn't know my worth. This was why I was seeing Mary as a dark silhouette. She was showing me that I wasn't fully present in myself. I wasn't embracing all of myself for myself. I wasn't living in full color.

I wasn't taking care of myself, and this was affecting my anxiety. Yes, I was eating healthfully and exercising, but I wasn't prioritizing my mental and spiritual health. I also compromised my physical health by doing so much for others to the point of exhaustion where I had no energy left for myself. I never prioritized my needs because I felt like I didn't deserve to since I didn't feel like I was enough.

However, during the month of May I started to see little glimmers of my worth and I began to see that I was enough. I gradually started to identify my needs. I learned to say "no" to others and "yes" to myself. I got comfortable investing in myself with time, money, and energy, knowing that I deserved this level of self-care. And by investing in myself, the universe has supported me and given me more too! I still slip up and fall into the pattern of taking care of my family first, but it's becoming easier for me to identify when I'm out of balance and need to return to myself and prioritize my needs. The next time I did the Mother Mary meditation, I saw Mary and Jesus again both in full color standing side-by-side.

What I learned with the support of Mary and am continuing to learn every day since is that you have to prioritize yourself. This means investing in yourself with time, money, and energy. The more steps you take to make yourself a priority, the more the universe matches that energy and invests in you. Spending time every day to do something you love is an investment. Spending money on yourself is an investment. I'm not talking about overspending beyond your means, but spending appropriate amounts of money on your hobbies, interests, and self-care. Spending money to receive quality emotional support is a healthy and worthwhile investment. You are enough and deserve to be seen, heard, and supported. You deserve to be true to yourself and not be who others want you to be. Not prioritizing your needs and being unseen and unheard mutes your light and feeds anxiety.

When you are healing, you need to heavily invest in yourself. If you have anxiety, especially debilitating anxiety, you have overdrawn your own energy reserves for others. It's time to replenish your energy and your essence and that starts with investing in yourself. As you fill yourself up and incorporate more joy into your life, you will begin to rewrite the old, outdated patterns that initially caused you anxiety. You'll start to create new healthy habits that are not only sustainable but help to end the cycles that only ever led you to not trust yourself.

YOUR WORTH

People with anxiety feel the adverse effects of the mental health stigma which propagates feelings of shame, affecting your self-worth. Feeling unworthy because you have anxiety only adds fuel to the raging fire that anxiety is. A low or non-existent self-worth causes you to hide your true self, your light. The truth is that you are worthy and everyone is. There is nothing you need to say or do to earn your worth. You are worthy and are loved unconditionally, just because. You must know your worth and fully embrace it in order to heal your anxiety. There's no other way around it.

There is a lot of information online and in books about how to boost your confidence, all of which seems futile to me until you know your worth. Without fully knowing and understanding your worth, confidence is like an empty shell. Confidence without self-worth is simply going through the motions without actually believing it in your core. However, confidence springs naturally when you embrace your self-worth. Once you know your worth, you become unshakable. When you know your worth and remember who you are at a soul level, your power can never be taken from you again.

My self-worth and confidence took massive hits during my 20-year struggle with anxiety. The stigma and harsh judgments from others left me feeling small, faulty, and lonely. My undiscovered self-worth was a huge impediment preventing me from healing. Since I didn't have an inkling of my self-worth, I didn't believe I deserved to prioritize myself—my self-care, my healing, or my mental health. I had to know and own my worth to feel confident enough to unapologetically shine my light and heal.

Fully embracing your worth is an internal job that can only be done by you. Even if someone were to tell you that you're worthy, it will never sink in until you believe it yourself. My introduction to my self-worth came from observing the animals in my life. They never seem to lose touch with the truth of their worth, knowing they deserve unconditional love, respect, and affection. My dog knows he deserves love no matter how stinky his breath is or how naughty he's been. However, I learned the most about my self-worth by observing the horses at my daughter's barn where they are pampered and nurtured. They get top of the line treatment including supplements, chiropractic care, and even monthly massages! I could clearly see how these beautiful creatures deserved this love and pampering. So why didn't I believe I deserved this level of care and compassion too?

Over time, the clear answer for me was to stop allowing external forces to dictate my value and self-worth. The noises and distractions around me had become so loud that I couldn't hear my own voice. By releasing toxic people and situations (see chapter three) I began to hear the whisperings of my own soul and these whisperings shed light on my worth. I had to embrace quietness and a certain amount of solitude so that I could listen to my heart and soul.

As I mentioned above, the people and situations who influenced my feelings of worth are irrelevant. Their opinions are just that—their opinions, and, over time, they lost their power over me. I learned that knowing and owning your self-worth is a precursor to reclaiming your power and using your voice (see chapter six). I gradually began to understand and know wholeheartedly I deserved the same amount of care and compassion as the horses at my daughter's barn. And you do too!

You might be wondering what exactly are you worthy of? Well, you're worthy of it all. Unconditional love, support, health, safety, comfort, success, and more. Knowing your worth is the catalyst to your healing. When you begin to know your worth, huge shifts will begin to take place on your journey.

Judgment and shame are very harsh energies in your body, and they severely impact your health. With anxiety, you already feel less than and undeserving. These feelings of unworthiness shut down the natural energy flow in your body and make you feel like you're under attack. You judge yourself because you have anxiety, yet judging yourself perpetuates anxiety. Judging and shaming yourself is very abrasive to your energy and is the equivalent to wearing clothes lined with sandpaper.

You most likely have already endured enormous amounts of judgments from friends, family, and society. You don't need to add to that and judge yourself too just because you have anxiety. Instead, radically accept yourself, anxiety and all and cultivate immovable self-worth. Anxiety may be a part of how you feel, but it doesn't define you! Embracing your self-worth is the missing piece that enables you to free yourself from anxiety and live your life authentically.

If I had a magic wand, I would wish for everyone reading this book to instantly know their worth wholeheartedly. Writing this book, I tried to think of ways to help you learn and understand your worth, but it's hard to teach because your worth is simply because you are. Then I remembered that my spirit team helped to spark my worth. And your spirit team is helping you too. The exercise below will help you on your path to discovering your worth with the support of your spirit team.

DISCOVERING YOUR WORTH EXERCISE

1. Trust Your Spirit Team

The first step in discovering your self-worth involves further trusting your spirit team (see chapter three). They will show you the people and situations that are adversely affecting your worth. Your spirit team wants the best situations and outcomes for you that support you here on earth and that will reflect your worth to you. It's hard to find your self-worth when you're around people or are in situations that want to keep your worth hidden. Trust the signs and messages you receive. Your spirit team will present you with better, more supportive opportunities. Trust that you deserve them.

2. *See Yourself with Angel Eyes*

The next step is to ask your spirit team to help you see yourself through their eyes, to see yourself as a child of God. Your angels love you unconditionally and see your inner and outer beauty. No harsh judgements, criticisms, or cruelty—only love, respect, and compassion. Welcoming their support in this way will shift how you see and feel about yourself overtime, nurturing your self-worth.

The seed that is your self-worth is already inside you and your spirit team is helping you to germinate that seed. Self-reflection and unearthing some deep-rooted beliefs around your worth will water your seed, helping it to grow and flourish.

INTERNAL SELF - WORTH BELIEFS

Many people hold onto beliefs that adversely affect their self-worth. Jim Kwik in his book, *Limitless*, calls them limiting beliefs because they limit you, keeping you contained in a metaphorical box while preventing you from living to your full potential. In his book, Kwik details three steps to uproot, disempower, and reframe limiting beliefs. These steps are: (1) name your limiting belief, (2) get to the facts, and (3) create a new belief.

Below I walk through the three-step process to undo the limiting beliefs that may be holding you back and keeping you small. These are just a sample of some of the beliefs that block out your light. As you go through these limiting beliefs, start to question how you would feel if you were able to release these limiting beliefs. What would your life look like if you embraced the new beliefs instead? Do you notice any subtle shifts/improvements to your anxiety just reading the new beliefs? Observe your self-talk and think about any additional limiting beliefs you carry around. Grab your journal and start exploring these beliefs.

1. Limiting Beliefs

- *I'm not good enough because I have anxiety.*
- *I have to earn love.*
- *I don't deserve peace of mind.*
- *I'm not worthy because I've made mistakes.*
- *I need to hide who I am since I'm not perfect.*
- *What other people think of me is important.*

2. Facts

All of these limiting beliefs are lies. They don't hold one ounce of truth. Some of these limiting beliefs may have felt true around some people in your life because they were pushing the narrative. But if you look closely, you'll see that these beliefs are false and are no longer part of your truth.

3. New Beliefs

- *I am good enough. Period. Anxiety does not define me.*
- *I deserve unconditional love.*
- *I choose peace.*
- *I am worthy because I am human. I make mistakes because I am human.*
- *I shine my light because I am perfectly imperfect.*
- *I value and prioritize my own thoughts and feelings.*

Your new beliefs won't limit you and instead will give you room to grow and to unapologetically shine your light freely. If you feel these new expansive beliefs help you, write them down and put them in a place where you will see them multiple times a day, every day. Include any other affirmations that feel empowering too. The more you read them out loud and/or read them quietly in your head, the more they will become part of your inner self-talk and will snuff out the limiting beliefs. You're rewiring your limiting beliefs and limiting self-talk. Over time, these affirmations will cement into your unconscious and start influencing your daily thoughts, decisions, and actions.

CANDY COATING

In the beginning of my third year in Angel Team, we studied an ascended master called El Morya. In Kyle Gray's Keepers of the Light oracle card deck, the El Morya card means "Awakening Presence," which I understand to mean as coming into your light. During the meditation we were guided to ask El Morya for guidance on any issues or concerns we had. Desperate, I asked for insight and guidance for my anxiety. My meditation with El Morya was very powerful and I got some clear answers. He showed me an image of a woman who had a candy coating shell on her, sort of like an M&M candy, but with a lot of cracks. These cracks were from the painful experiences in her life that contributed to her growth— some dark night of the soul experiences. This cracked exterior candy coating wasn't necessarily bad either. It was a helpful form of protection at some point, an armor. It just wasn't helping her anymore and was actually hurting her. What was most remarkable about the image I saw was the beautiful light that was shining through the cracks in her candy coating.

The woman in the image was hunched over, almost like she had a stomachache. When I tuned into the image more closely, I realized that the woman was hunched over because of fear. She was afraid of the candy coating coming off. She was doing her best to keep this cracked armor in place so that it could continue to contain her light. Her light was getting so strong that the candy coating had not only cracked but was getting ready to pop off soon. Her candy shell could no longer stay on because of the high vibrational frequency of her light. This woman's light needed to shine, but the initial vulnerability and rawness she would inevitably feel when she exposed her light terrified her. This woman was me and she's all of us with anxiety.

This image sums up what people with anxiety experience. For too long you have been understandably hiding and dimming your light out of fear: fear of persecution, fear of being ridiculed, or fear of being alone, or maybe all of these reasons. However, as I've described throughout this chapter, dimming your light creates anxiety. Actively trying to contain your light, your essence, and denying yourself the freedom of self-expression suffocates your soul. Your soul needs room to expand and breathe.

My vision showed me that anxiety is hiding your light, your true self, and your soul. Trying to dim the light within you to fit in or to keep the peace destroys your self-trust. Not honoring your soul creates an internal conflict, feeding distrust in your body which produces adrenaline and fuels anxiety. Instead of the energy flowing freely throughout your body, the energy of your soul hits a roadblock and since your light cannot be fully expressed, it surfaces as anxiety.

With the candy coating on, you're figuratively asleep, buying into the beliefs that you're not good enough. You're stuck in The Matrix, living someone else's narrative. The candy coating is all of the limiting beliefs you've been carrying around that are hurting you physically, emotionally, and spiritually. Anxiety is your body's clear signal that it's time to "awaken" at a soul level; it's time to shine your light.

Connecting to El Morya, I learned that to heal anxiety, you must completely embrace and step into your light. Your fears will still be there, but as you regularly step into your light, your fears will eventually subside. Stepping into your light will shed light on your fears so that they no longer have power over you. It's time for you to shed your candy coating and unapologetically shine your light. It's time to stand tall and confidently in your beautiful light, to only move forward, grounded in your light. And as you shine your light, you set off a chain reaction for others to do the same.

BRINGING OUR FEARS INTO THE LIGHT

People hide their light for different reasons, fear being the common cause. It's understandable. Hiding your true self makes you feel safe and appeases your fears temporarily. It did for me. But if you have anxiety, dimming your light isn't working anymore. Your soul is demanding that you take center stage of your life.

The fears you have of shining your light are very real and should not be taken lightly. These fears most likely helped protect you at some point in your life. However, anxiety is an indicator that it's time to bring your fears into the light. You must address your fears about being seen and heard so that you can move through them. You need to identify where in your life you're hiding your light and why you're doing it. It's completely normal to have fears, but you must acknowledge them to disempower them. Addressing your fears head on, you'll be able to move past them.

Below I've outlined three steps to help you acknowledge, track down the source, and move through your fears. I go through examples of different fears about shining your light throughout the exercise. Jot down in your journal which fears resonate with you and any additional fears you have. Writing down your fears is not only a release in itself, but also brings clarity as to why you are hiding your light.

THREE STEPS TO DISEMPOWER YOUR FEARS

1. Be honest about your what your fears are.

Think about shining your light, living your life authentically, and openly expressing your true self. Take note of any fears that come up and be clear and specific about what you're actually afraid of. There's no right or wrong answers here. Whatever your fears are, there is no shame in them. Just be honest about what you're afraid of. Truthfully acknowledging your fears paves the way for you to safely explore and disempower them.

Examples of Fears Around Shining Your Light

- I will be laughed at.
- Nobody will like the real me.
- I will be criticized.
- I will be ostracized.
- I will be alone.

2. Track down the source of your fears.

Hone in on the people or events that have shaped your fears. Explore and be honest about the source. Was it an event from your childhood? Was it programming from your parents? Was it something you experienced as an adult? Identifying where your fears originated helps to put them into context. Your fears no longer have that tight grip on you when you are able to track down the source. You're also better equipped to protect yourself and create boundaries that help you feel safe (see chapter six).

Examples of Fears

- I will be laughed at. As a child, I was laughed at for the clothes I liked to wear.
- Nobody will like the real me. People say I'm weird when I share my true self with them.
- I will be criticized. My teachers criticized me for being different.

- I will be ostracized. I was not included in certain groups/activities at school/work when I was shining my light.
- I will be alone. My parents shunned me when I stopped doing what they wanted me to do and started doing what lit me up.

3. Apply worst case scenarios to your fears.

You have so much to gain in shining your light, so think about what's the worst case scenario that could happen if your fears actualized. In this step, you'll move through and explore how much you would really lose if your fears happened. The purpose of this exercise is to show you that while your fears are very real and legitimate, your worst case scenarios may not be that bad and could, in fact, set you free.

Worst Case Scenario Examples

- *You get laughed at for shining your light:* While it's hurtful to be laughed at, now you know that this person or these people are not part of your support crew. You can choose to create solid boundaries with these people or release them to protect you and your light.
- *Nobody likes the real you:* When you start to step into your light, many people won't like you. This really isn't about you though. You shining your light highlights how these people are choosing to

live small and not step into their own light. You embracing your power is threatening to some people. You're shining your light for yourself and your own healing. It's OK if others don't like the real you.

- *I will be criticized:* Anyone who criticizes you for stepping into your light and power doesn't deserve you. Most likely they will criticize you whether or not you embrace your true self. Sadly, these people will not support your growth and healing and are not good for you.

- *I will be ostracized:* Yes, you will probably be ostracized for honestly expressing yourself. Is it better to dim your light in order to fit into certain groups or live freely with a much smaller but sturdier support crew? As I talked about in chapter three, when you're doing the inner work and healing yourself your circle of support gets smaller. This is normal. Fewer quality relationships are more supportive than many more casual and conditional relationships. Holding onto anything or anyone out of fear never works out.

- *I will be alone:* Being ostracized and subsequently alone can feel very uncomfortable, but time alone can also be very healing. Without all of the external distractions, you can tune into yourself and focus on your healing. Embrace your alone time and treasure it. New friendships will eventually develop. When you know your worth and step into your light, your new relationships will mirror this energy too. It's better to be alone than with someone who won't accept you with your light turned on.

"It's our light, not our darkness that most frightens us."

— MARIANNE WILLIAMSOM, A RETURN
TO LOVE

There's truth in this quote because opening yourself up to shine your light requires a certain amount of vulnerability. As you begin to shine your light, you have to face your fears and your darkness. Shedding light on the reasons you're hiding your light is tough soul work. Know that facing your fears and moving through them is the path to living authentically and honoring your soul. Moving through your fears will free you to shine your light and free you from anxiety.

SELF - MORE INSTEAD OF SELF - LESS

I'll never forget an offhanded comment a flippant relative said shortly after my husband and I got married more than 20 years ago. She told me that during her free time she liked to think of ways she could be a better wife to her husband. Already trained to read between the lines of passive aggressive narcissistic comments, I understood the underlying message of her barb. She felt I was investing too much in myself and should instead strive to be selfless and put my husband's needs before my own. Got it!

The definition of selfish implies that I was thinking of just myself without regard for anyone else. This woman was barely around us to know if I was being selfish; she only knew the highlights of our lives. At that point I was a newlywed, moving around for my husband's military career, and working a full-time job as I worked on my master's degree. The definition of selfless means to be unconcerned about yourself. As the word spells out, you are less of yourself, self-less. This woman wanted me to dim my light and I did for a while. I made myself small so that she and others felt better about their own choices to live small.

To restore your health, it's important to be able to identify when someone is invalidating you and/or pushing you to dim your light. Is someone suggesting you be yourself less? Do they want you to pass on your dreams in order to make their complacency seem acceptable? Is someone telling you that you shouldn't stand up for yourself? That you should put your own needs and self-care on the back burner? If you're answering yes to any of these questions, it's time to put the brakes on in those relationships and redirect your attention back to yourself.

While I don't condone selfishness, acting selflessly isn't the answer either. Being yourself more is not the same as being selfish. Someone who is selfish acts only on their own behalf without consideration of anyone else.

You should only ever embrace your "self-more." Self-more acknowledges others to the point of not losing yourself and your inner peace for another person. It's knowing who you are, what your needs, wants, and dreams are and prioritizing them. Without being yourself more, you're just a shell of who you are to others and yourself. Anyone who truly values you wants the most authentic version of yourself. No exceptions.

When this woman said this comment to me about finding ways to be a better wife, I didn't know what to think. It was so weird and outdated that I couldn't make sense of it. Even though she seemed pleased with her words, I was confused. Did it change my day-to-day behavior? No. However, whenever I was around her, I dimmed my light because I knew she disapproved of me.

I can now see how much she needed me to be myself less so that she could feel better about herself. Having goals and working hard to achieve them did not make me selfish. She needed to place that label on me so that she could feel better for limiting herself and not following through with her own dreams. She wanted to drop a hint that I was not a good enough wife and that being myself less would be more beneficial for my husband, when in fact we decided to marry each other when we were both fully ourselves, with no dimming at all.

Anxiety is your soul's way of saying it's time to be your "self-more" and to know deep in your heart your self-worth and that you are enough. It is telling you to return to yourself, to invest in yourself, love yourself, and accept yourself as you are. It means you should do what brings you joy and fills up your heart and courageously step into your light, living your life boldly. And by the way, being self-less didn't work for this woman either. She and her husband are no longer together.

SELF - LOVE

Self-love is the third part of your solid foundation. Embracing your worth and knowing you're enough are needed to foster self-love. Self-love is nurturing yourself holistically. It's loving yourself as you are today and every day. It's believing in yourself, trusting your intuition and voice. Self-love allows you to create loving boundaries to protect yourself and your energy (see chapter six).

Love is the panacea for fear. Love is stronger than fear, so when we approach life from a place of self-love, fear is muscled out. This is why self-love heals anxiety. Radically embracing self-love effortlessly eradicates fear.

Like many of my life lessons, I learned a lot about self-love through parenting my kids. I started to notice a discrepancy between how I allowed others to treat me versus my kids. I would let others overstep my boundaries and drain my energy, but I would be fiercely protective of my kids' boundaries. As my anxiety started to heal, I was able to see the difference. Just being aware of the difference helped me support and nurture myself from a place of self-love. My self-love has set the bar for other relationships in my life too.

Below is an exercise to help you to tune into what self-love feels like. The more you tune into divine love and self-love, the easier it becomes to make daily decisions from a place of love instead of fear. I recommend doing this exercise daily until your foundation is solidified.

Self - Love Exercise

Sit comfortably in a quiet spot and focus on your breathing. After a few minutes, focus on your heart chakra (in the middle of your chest). Invite divine love into your heart and observe how it feels. Then welcome your spirit team to guide you in nurturing self-love. Write down anything that comes up for you.

The divine love you felt is what your self-love should feel like. Your daily actions and choices should leave you feeling in alignment with divine love. Ask yourself: How can I treat myself as I would my own child or someone I deeply love? Do I treat myself with love and tenderness? Am I fiercely protective of myself? What are some ways I can foster self-love?

TRUST YOUR LIGHT

I lived in the shadows for years, hiding my light to placate my fears. I carried the fearful programming I learned as a child, with me as an adult. In order for my fears to stop running me, I had to stop running from them. I gave myself permission to feel my fears and explore them. I lived through my worst-case scenarios to discover that my worst cases in reality weren't that bad.

As I began to prioritize my physical and mental health and started shining my light, many of my relationships (business, family, and friends) dropped off. When I embraced my spiritual side, even more relationships dissolved. Now I invest my time and energy into myself, my healing, and the relationships that are dear to me. My time alone without distractions created space for me to learn how to value and prioritize myself. I learned that I am enough—there is nothing I need to do or prove. I also learned that I'm worthy of beauty, magic, blessings, and abundance just because I'm alive.

Hiding your light is no longer serving you. Just as a flower needs sunlight in order to bloom, your light is needed in order for your soul to grow. You are safe to shine your light and deserve to honor your soul. Follow your own path, knowing you don't have to be who others want you to be. Know and trust that you and your light are enough.

Shining your light is about honestly and authentically expressing yourself. It's about being free to remove all of your masks and live in honest alignment with your soul. Trusting your light and shining it is not done for attention or for any other outcome than to free yourself. Your light gets switched on when you know your worth and know you are enough. Boldly stepping into your light and trusting it is an act of bravery and allows deep healing to take place.

Your light is your internal guide. It will highlight the path you need to take to heal yourself. Your light and your path will look different than everyone else's, as will the timing of your healing. Trust your own light and your own unique healing journey it sets you on.

5

I TRUST THE RHYTHM OF MY SOUL

"To live is to be musical, starting with the blood dancing in your veins. Everything living has a rhythm. Do you feel your music?"

— MICHAEL JACKSON

YOU CAME INTO THIS WORLD WITH A SOUL. YOUR SOUL IS your pure essence, and it can never be destroyed. It's what makes you who you are—your likes, dislikes, passions, gifts, talents, and more. Your soul knows what is best for you at all times. It knows what you need and what you should avoid. It knows what will heal you and what detracts from you. Living from your soul, honoring its rhythms, and trusting them is the recipe for soul freedom and freedom from anxiety.

Your soul craves freedom. Freedom to express itself, however that looks for you. Freedom from the expectations of others—the freedom to breathe. Soul freedom will help you heal and grow during your lifetime. Your soul is an etheric vessel that contains infinite wisdom, knowledge, and divine strength. It knows the direction you need to go and the steps you must take in order to live freely.

Most people are trained from infancy to tune out their souls. It's ingrained from an early age to ignore the directions and cues from your intuition and instead shift your focus to everything that's outside of you. You've been taught to live as a human with the world living inside of you, instead of as a human living in the world. This is overwhelming and overpowering. It separates you from your soul, drowning out who you really are. You forget what brings you joy, what excites you, and what strengthens you. As you begin to remove any and all barriers between you and your soul, you can start hearing your soul again so that you can live a soul-led life.

Many people are asleep in their lives. They go through the motions of their daily lives without really knowing why they're doing it. They're on autopilot, doing things (or not doing things) because that's what they've always done (or not done) without questioning if what they're doing (or not doing) is, in fact, right for them. Tuning into your soul's rhythm is an invitation to deeply know yourself and to live your life purposely for your nourishment, growth, and joy.

Throughout this book I talk about traveling your own unique healing path that is meant for you. Your path that allows you to live in alignment with your soul while healing anxiety. It is a path that speaks and resonates with you, a path that feels right even though it may seem illogical or scary. This chapter is about following your path, a path that was only ever meant for you and trusting where it leads you—trusting the rhythm of your soul.

RHYTHM AROUND AND WITHIN YOU

Dictionary.com defines rhythm as "movement or procedure with uniform or patterned recurrence of a beat, accent, or the like." Most people can easily identify rhythm in music, but if you pay close attention, you'll see that the natural world around you has rhythms that affect everyday life. Nature exhibits her own rhythms daily and yearly. Nature's rhythms are concentric with the earth's cycles and connected to the sun's and moon's rhythms. The earth's rotations in conjunction with the sun and moon create a recurring pattern in nature's yearly seasons —fall, winter, spring, summer where I live and dry seasons and rainy seasons in other parts of the world. Additionally, the earth, sun, and moon connection shows daily rhythms and patterns such as sunlight and warmer temperatures during the day and moonlight and cooler temperatures at nights. There is also a rhythmic ebb and flow of the ocean's waves and tides that are strongly connected to both the sun's and moon's rhythms.

There's rhythm in the flora and fauna that responds to nature's rhythms, helping them adapt to hot and cold temperatures, wet and dry climates, best times to forage or hunt, and when to reproduce. For example, many flowers exhibit nyctinasty, where they rhythmically close themselves at night to protect themselves from predators, safeguarding successful pollination. Trees drop their leaves every fall season to ensure their survival during the colder months. Some wildlife hibernate during the winter while others migrate. There is rhythm in the natural world all around us.

As in nature, there's an inherent rhythm to your days, weeks, months, and year. There's a rhythm to your mornings, afternoons, and evenings. Your body has its own unique rhythms, from the rhythmic beating of your heart to the rhythm of your sleep cycles. These rhythms are cyclical and at the same time are changing. Nature and wildlife demonstrate how important it is to honor the rhythms around you and inside you to not only survive but also thrive. Tuning into your body's natural rhythms ensures that you know what your needs are so that you are caring for yourself in such a way that allows your body to flourish.

SOUL RHYTHM

Just as in nature, where every living thing has its own signature cadence, so do people. I call it soul rhythm. Your soul's rhythm is what you need physically, emotionally, and spiritually at any given time to thrive. It's the changes you need to make and the hurdles you need to jump for your growth and healing.

The rhythm of your soul is like a flowing body of water—
a river, stream, creek, or maybe a combination of all three.
Your river or stream is your healing journey, your unique
and individual path through life. The bends and curves in
your stream are where your path pivots to be in better
alignment with your soul. Your soul rhythm, like a river or
stream will flow quickly sometimes and barely move at
others. Healing and growth are occurring at both speeds
and both are a necessary part of your soul's rhythm and
needed for your evolution.

Soul rhythm is the directional cues from your soul letting
you know where to go, what to do, and what you need at
any given time. Tuning into your soul's rhythm means
listening to when you need to hunker down and take a
breather and when to step out because it's your time to
bloom. Just as nature does, your soul rhythm takes into
account the times you're experiencing rapid growth and
the times you need to rest and integrate. Your soul rhythm
nudges you when it's time to speak up, when it's better to
listen, when to work your butt off, when to recuperate,
when to forge ahead, and when to wait it out. Soul rhythm
is heeding your intuition about when to walk, run, sit, and
at times, when to dance.

Trusting your soul's rhythm is dancing with the universe.
The beats from your soul are guiding you towards an
authentic life individually tailored to you. A life that's an
extension of your soul. You're doing the tango with the
subtle and sometimes not so subtle whispers, shouts, and
cries of your soul that are the sacred communion between
your mind, body, soul, and the universe. You're listening

deeply to what you need to nourish your mind, body, and soul from day to day and sometimes minute to minute and continually adapting to ensure your needs are met.

Trusting your soul's rhythm is about listening deeply to your intuition and going forward with what feels right even though it may not make sense in the moment. For example, I received the title of this chapter in a dream from my angels and spirit team. I instantly knew it needed a place in my book even though I wasn't entirely clear what soul rhythm meant. I even wrote a tentative first draft of this chapter knowing it wasn't quite right. According to my soul's rhythm, I soon got the lessons and information I needed to rewrite this chapter and convey the message the best that I could. I trusted my dream and my intuition to include this chapter. I trusted the rhythm of my soul and I'm so glad I did because this chapter was so deep, introspective, and fun to write.

Trusting the rhythm of your soul is going with the flow of your life. Trusting your soul's rhythm is honoring the twists, turns, bumps, and jumps in your healing journey instead of trying to force your stream to flow straight. Resisting the rhythm of your soul is like trying to swim upstream. It's much easier to embrace the flow of your soul, with all of its meanders and bends, instead of trying to force goals, agendas, or timelines that don't fit you.

Trusting your soul's unique rhythm is about turning your focus inward, becoming intrinsically motivated, listening to what your mind, body, and soul needs. You become so tuned in with yourself that you're no longer affected by the external noise around you. You prioritize what's best for you, your health, and mental wellness. You make choices that bring you joy and comfort instead of what family, friends, or society say you should do. Trusting your soul's rhythm is about honoring and nourishing your mind, body, and spirit for your growth.

GASLIGHTING YOUR SOUL

It's not your fault you have anxiety because it's been ingrained in you since you were young to trust everyone but yourself, from your family, friends, teachers, doctors, religious leaders, society, institutions, and the media. You've been programmed to walk someone else's path even though your soul requires you to travel your own unique path that's only meant for you. Some people may have similar journeys, but no two paths will be completely the same.

Your anxiety is alerting you that something around you is suffocating your soul. Anxiety is actually like the canaries in the coal mines that alerted the miners when there were toxins in the air. Canaries are more sensitive than humans and died when exposed to smaller amounts of methane and carbon monoxide that weren't yet fatal to humans in these quantities but which would eventually become fatal with continued exposure. Like the canaries, people with anxiety are more sensitive than others and are detecting dysfunction. Anxiety is your body and soul's way of sending you SOS signals that you've been exposed to soul toxins.

Anxiety is the telltale sign that you're ignoring your soul's rhythm and ultimately gaslighting your soul, compromising your soul's freedom. Overriding the signals from your soul is harmful and will lead you down a path that's not meant for you. Gaslighting your soul inhibits your soul expression, affecting your health and mental wellness.

NARATIVES

Most people have lost touch with who they are at a soul level. There is a flood of narratives about what people should do, say, feel, look like, want, and so on. All of this noise is distracting and keeps you from hearing your own soul. All the false narratives, figurative boxes, and outdated constructs severely impact your life, leaving you feeling like a shell of yourself, energetically starved and depleted because you're not fueling yourself physically, emotionally, and spiritually as you need to in order to feel your best and live your fullest life.

> *"They're just culturally constructed, artificial, ever-changing cages created to maintain institutions. It struck me that in every family, culture, or religion, ideas of right and wrong are the hot cattle prods, the barking sheep dogs that keep the masses in their herd. They are the bars that keep us caged."*

> — GLENNON DOYLE, UNTAMED

Glennon Doyle's quote from her book, *Untamed*, perfectly describes the dysfunctional narratives about shoulds and shouldn'ts, good and bad, and right and wrong.

When I refer to narratives, I'm talking about the stories, beliefs, and truths that people believe about themselves and the world around them. Narratives define how people perceive and remember different experiences or events. It's important to remember that other people's narratives are their own interpretations and aren't necessarily true or more importantly, not true for you. Anxiety is compounded when you unknowingly confuse other people's narratives as your own and uphold their beliefs and truths. This is the crux of my definition of anxiety: *unconsciously and continually gaslighting yourself in order to make yourself small to accommodate others.*

What you need to thrive is different from everyone else, but you've learned to ignore your own needs and instead get caught up in what you "should" need, how you "should" feel, and what your dreams "should" look like. As I mentioned in chapter three, the external noises and narratives surrounding you can get very loud. So loud that they drown out your own inner voice, your soul, so that you sooner or later unconsciously and continually conform to these narratives that were never yours.

You become like a memory foam mattress where you distort and conform yourself to narratives that are not your own. Beliefs and narratives from people, institutions, and society change you as you unintentionally adopt these beliefs as your own. Note that memory foam mattresses never expand, only contracting and molding to whoever is closest to it, the person who sleeps on it the most. Similarly, adopting the narratives of others will diminish you, never properly nourishing you so that you can expand and grow according to your soul rhythm.

People are accustomed to the narratives that have been ingrained in them, completely destroying their self-trust. The loss of self-trust forces many to automatically and repeatedly seek out the advice of others instead of turning within themselves to find the answers they need from their souls. They are peppering in more noises and distractions rather than snuffing them out so as to better hear their own voices and internal infinite wisdom. It's not bad to discuss important matters with a trusted friend. In fact, I believe sharing and unpacking some important decisions with someone close to you is very helpful as long as you trust your own inner guidance first and foremost, and the other person serves more as a sounding board instead of an expert.

Below are some examples of narratives I believed to be my own. I absorbed these narratives from a combination of all of the sources I mentioned above starting from childhood and continuing as an adult.

Examples of Extrinsic Narratives

- It's important to dress well to impress others.
- The grades I get in school determine if I'm smart.
- My teachers know who's going to be successful.

- I need to spend time with friends to have a good time.
- My worth is determined by how much money I make.
- My worth is determined by how much higher education I have.
- I must work to be deserving of love.
- To be strong, I have to do everything on my own.
- I'm selfish when I prioritize my own needs.

These narratives were implied through the words and actions from external sources and pulled me out of myself. Instead of being driven from my soul, I was taking my cues from the world around me. Adhering to the false narratives around me robbed me of my power. The noises and distractions were calling the shots for me. On my healing journey I was able to over time identify the false narratives I was holding close to me and unravel all of the ways I was unconsciously and continually gaslighting my soul. I learned to tune in and hear what my soul believed. Below are the intrinsic narratives I consciously chose to adopt that reframed the extrinsic narratives I unknowingly upheld.

Examples of Intrinsic Narratives

- I dress to feel good for myself.
- The education system does not define my intelligence; I do.

- My teachers are human like me and are in charge of their own trajectory, not mine.
- I have fun alone and with my friends.
- Money is an important part of my life, but it doesn't define me.
- I enjoy learning, but a higher education doesn't define me.
- I always deserve love. There's nothing I need to do or prove to receive love.
- It's OK to ask for help. Asking for help is not a weakness.
- My needs are important and deserve to be prioritized.

I've mentioned throughout this book that anxiety is your body's way of trying to get your attention, which your body has to do when you're living with someone else's truth instead of your own. Since anxiety is loud and uncomfortable, it gets your attention. You can't ignore anxiety. You can't push anxiety aside. You can't gaslight anxiety. Anxiety makes itself known. Anxiety is telling you to start writing your own script and narrating your own life. Anxiety demands that you take back the reins and reclaim your power. This is how anxiety heals.

You're asleep when you live your life according to parameters set by others. You're going through the motions, but you're not connected to your body or soul, and it affects your mind. You're extrinsically motivated instead of intrinsically focused. Your soul is desperate to reconnect with your mind and body. Your soul wants to lead the way so that you can live your life free and on your terms.

Other people's narratives can be so deeply ingrained, you may not recognize that you've adopted them. It will take time and a lot of introspection to initially identify these narratives and even more time to unravel their effects. Below are some tips that will help you decipher these narratives.

- A narrative that is someone else's will make you feel small, weak, and less than most of the time. You and your needs will feel neither valid nor important.
- A narrative that is your own will make you feel strong and empowered. You and your needs will be both seen and heard.

Narratives Journal Prompts

The journal prompts below will help you begin to uncover the narratives that are shaping your life and uproot the ones that aren't yours. Take your time answering the questions and come back to them frequently as the veils in your life continue to be lifted.

- Which intrinsic beliefs do you hold that cause you to feel bad about yourself? Where did these narratives originate? From you or from external sources? Why do you think these narratives were pushed on you? How can you reframe these beliefs to be supportive of you?

- Which intrinsic beliefs do you hold that make you feel good about yourself? Where did these narratives originate from? From you or from external sources? Do these beliefs originate from your self-worth and self-love (intrinsic) or do these beliefs make you feel like you have to earn your worth and love (extrinsic)? Do you need to reframe these beliefs for your healing, growth, and soul expansion?
- Review your daily, weekly, monthly, and yearly routines. How do they make you feel? Do you do them because you want to or because you feel like you should do them?

COMPARING

How many times do you compare yourself to others, gauging your worth off their successes or failures? I definitely have! Who's more successful? Who's thinner? Whose kids are better behaved? Who makes more money? Who's got the bigger house? Who has a more prestigious job?

Comparing yourself is a result of the narratives you've been told and is completely normal. Extrinsic narratives generally instill fear and insecurity in people, resulting in comparison. People are wired to compare themselves to others as a way to measure themselves. They compare themselves to ensure they're staying in their figurative boxes.

The unconscious act of comparing runs deep inside everyone, coming from an energy and mindset of scarcity or lack. When unchecked and unfiltered, comparing shifts into the dysfunctional labeling of "haves" and "have nots." In other words, people become obsessed with comparing themselves to others and begin to see themselves as either having more or having less than others. Some people even go as far as to consider themselves better (or worse) than others based on their comparisons.

A few years ago, my husband and I went out to dinner with another couple we had recently met. I was having a good time enjoying the new restaurant, the food, and the adult conversation as my kids were home with a sitter. Towards the end of the night, the wife interrupted mid-conversation, reminding me that I was older than her. Weird, right? I'm not sure if she was trying to feel better about herself, saying that she was younger or if she felt like she was better than me and felt she needed to put me in my place. Either way, as I was enjoying myself, the company, the atmosphere, and the food, she probably wasted her entire child-free evening comparing herself.

This couple, who we eventually stopped getting together with, obsessively compared themselves to not just us but others too. At that time, they considered us the "have nots." They desperately needed us to be the "have nots" so that they could feel better about themselves. They needed to feel like they had more money, a bigger house, better jobs, more of everything so that they could sleep at night knowing that they were ahead of someone else.

Even though comparing is normal, you can stop it from controlling you. Being aware that you're comparing yourself is a huge first step to tuning into the rhythm of your soul. Remember that your journey through life will be different than everyone else. Not only will success look different for you than it will for others, but the timing of your success will also be different. There IS enough abundance for you and others to both be the "haves" and be successful.

People compare themselves because they've been taught to be like everyone else and see themselves as part of a collective. They have been taught to not stick out. To blend in and hide their true self and instead differentiate themselves based off lofty parameters like income, appearances, houses, and cars. Propaganda from the media and the education system constantly bombards you with narratives that says everyone's the same and to group everyone together collectively instead of seeing each person as a beautiful unique individual who complements others and society well with the unique talents and attributes they contribute. You've learned to suppress your needs, dreams, and passions in order to fit in. You've been programmed to seek out acceptance and approval like a thirsty person seeks the rare pool of water while stuck in a desert.

Comparing Journal Prompts

Don't judge yourself if you're comparing. It's completely normal. Just being aware of when you're doing it is enough to dismantle the effects of comparing. The journal prompts below will help to bring further insights into your comparisons.

- In what areas of your life do you compare yourself to others?
- When you compare yourself, do you feel better or worse about yourself?
- Were you happy with yourself before the comparison?
- Are you happy with the big picture of your life instead of the singular area you are comparing?

NORMALCY AND CONFORMING

Another reason people compare themselves is to ensure that they're "normal." People feel comforted knowing that they're not veering too far off track. They want to make sure that they're not way ahead or too far behind because they want to blend in.

The desire for normalcy is a defensive tactic. Normal means you're accepted, you have friends, and people like you. Therefore, you're not a target of gossip, ridicule, or bullying. Most people only want to associate with others who are like them because they are perceived as predictable and safe. Throughout history, the unknown and being different has always terrified people and caused some groups of people to do horrific things. However, hiding and gaslighting your soul for the safety and security of social acceptance is hurting you today. It's causing you anxiety and showing you that fitting in is neither safe nor secure. Normalcy gives the illusion of safety, but at what expense?

Dictionary.com defines normal as;

> *"conforming to the standard or the common type."*

Conforming to anything requires you to change yourself, from the clothes you wear, the car you drive, the clubs or sports you participate in, the friends you chose, and your dreams and aspirations. You're out of rhythm with your soul when you change yourself for the benefit of other people, institutions, and cultures.

Historically, people had to conform to be part of a community in order to survive. Conformity meant safety and security, but this is no longer the case. I believe that at this point in time, conforming is doing more harm than good. Conforming is so deeply ingrained that it's terrifying to even think about walking your own path, yet that's the very thing you need to do to heal and thrive. You no longer live in times where your livelihood is in jeopardy when you don't conform and are safe to wholly seize your individuality. Everyone's unique characteristics collectively will strengthen and solidify communities.

"If you are always trying to be normal you will never know how amazing you can be."

— *MAYA ANGELOU*

Striving for normalcy sounds comforting in theory, but there's a downside. You become so invested in other's opinions of you that you lose touch with your own feelings and sense of self. Your dreams get downgraded when you prioritize your need for normalcy. You're gaslighting your soul when normalcy is what you aspire for. I know from experience.

Back in the 80s and early 90s my childhood was very unconventional. With divorced parents and my Panamanian heritage, I did not fit in. It was clear to me from a young age that I was nowhere near normal, yet normalcy is what I craved. As a teenager and young adult my desire for normalcy was my primary motivator for so many of my pursuits. Years later, when I was a newlywed, a woman approached me at a family gathering and arrogantly referred to her own family as "a happy normal family." This stung because she knew my family background. She added salt to my wound.

I now know the normalcy I craved as a young girl and young adult doesn't exist. The truth is being different is normal. I don't try to be different just for the sake of coming across as quirky. I just do what feels right to me. I've learned to become comfortable in my own skin.

Chasing down normalcy depletes your essence, dulling you and stifling your soul. A life curated to look like those around you stunts your growth and healing. Your uniqueness and individuality are what's normal. To heal from the inside out you have to take the road less traveled. Your mental health demands it!

Others may judge you for being "weird" or "strange," but their judgments are more of a reflection of themselves than of you. Your flair might ruffle their squareness. In all honesty, the people who judge you for being different will judge you no matter what you do, so you might as well be yourself. If you have to hide or change who you are in order for others to like you, then they are not for you. Their opinions of you matter least.

Reflecting on that woman's comment 20 years later has been revealing. At the time I believed her that her family was normal and happy. However, with time, experience, and multiple veils removed, I now see that her family is extremely unhealthy and dysfunctional. My family of origin's dysfunction was on full display whereas this woman's crippling family dynamics were concealed and hidden behind the "happy normal family" mask. At least part of what she said was the truth—her dysfunctional family is normal.

Normality and Conforming Journal Prompts

Striving for normalcy dulls your light, preventing you from living your fullest life. The journal prompts below will help you pinpoint the ways you may be conforming yourself in order to be normal and blend in. The questions will also help get you thinking about expressing your true self.

- How do you seek out normalcy and how does it make you feel safe?
- Have you changed who you are to feel normal? How?
- Are there certain aspects of yourself that you're hiding? Describe them.
- Is there anything different about you that you're embarrassed about? Describe it.
- How can you embrace your individuality in a way that feels safe for you? Explain.

BELONGING VERSUS FITTING IN

Normalcy becomes the focus when the goal is to fit in. Fitting in and normalcy go hand-in-hand, providing the semblance of safety in numbers. It's ingrained in people to want to belong to a crowd, group, and/or community. It's natural to pursue social connections because they can benefit your physical health and mental wellness. But when you're required to change and compromise who you are at your core for acceptance, are these social connections still supportive?

> "Fitting in is about assessing a situation and becoming who you need to be to be accepted. Belonging on the other hand, doesn't require us to change who we are; it requires us to be who we are."

— BRENÉ BROWN, *THE GIFTS OF IMPERFECTION*

Fitting in requires you to change yourself, like a chameleon, according to the norms and expectations specific to each group. As you know, changing yourself and gaslighting your soul impacts your mental health. Just like a bicycle, the wheels, chains, and gears that need to connect at the right time to function optimally get thrown out of whack when you gaslight your soul for the benefit of others. Chains slip, wheels fall off, and the gears stick. You're not grounded or connected to yourself. You're out of rhythm with your soul.

Some people do whatever it takes to fit in. Some become easygoing. There are clear messages from our culture, media, friends, and family that easygoing is a personality trait everyone should strive for. However, easygoing is synonymous with losing yourself. You're shutting down certain aspects of yourself when you lack boundaries, don't speak up for yourself, and forgo what's in your best interest in order to fit in. The media never depicts the fun popular people as the ones who are diligent about taking care of their needs. The ones who are secure enough in themselves that they're comfortable upholding their boundaries when they need to. The likable characters instead are the ones who are seen as easygoing.

When you have anxiety, your needs have to come first. You have to be safely and solidly grounded in yourself before you can share of yourself with any group, community, or gathering. You have to belong to yourself and be committed to doing what's right for you instead of following the masses. And you'll ONLY share of yourself and your gorgeous light when it's a group that feels right for you. Where you feel seen, heard, and valued.

Not fitting in has always been my normal. I've never known any different. During our time moving every two to three years as a military family, I would have loved to fit in with the communities where I lived, as well as with the other military spouses. However, I wasn't willing to compromise myself or my beliefs.

The beauty of not fitting in is that I never felt the false security of fitting in. This gave me a certain amount of freedom. Freedom to do what I wanted because I was free from the expectations of others. Sometimes it's necessary to bravely stand on your own, so that you can live your own truth. To relieve yourself of the burden of worrying about what other people think or want.

In each new town we moved to, I would have loved to find my people, a group where I belonged. Instead, I learned that belonging only comes from within. Belonging is a spiritual journey to radically accepting yourself. If you know your self-worth, engage in self-love, and accept yourself as you are, then you will belong no matter where you go. When you are comfortable with yourself and enjoy time by yourself, you belong to yourself—the best kind of belonging.

When you radically accept yourself and belong to yourself, you start to attract people and situations where you are accepted as yourself. The universe matches your energy, and you start attracting people and opportunities that uphold you. However, since you only ever belong to yourself, true belonging starts and stops with you.

Belonging Versus Fitting In Journal Prompts

The journal prompts below are to help you dig deep and uncover any ways you may be changing yourself to fit in with others. There are no wrong answers, so be honest with yourself. Your honest answers will help you to shift your focus from fitting in to cultivating a belonging to yourself.

- Do you feel like you fit in or belong? If so, how?
- Does not fitting in make you feel uncomfortable? How?
- Do you go to great lengths to try to fit in? Describe them.
- Do you compromise any aspect of yourself or your beliefs to be part of any group? How?
- How would it feel to be yourself in different social situations?

PEOPLE PLEASING

A combination of not knowing your worth and gaslighting your soul results in a debilitating people pleasing pattern that has detrimental effects on your health and mental wellness. Low self-worth, which I covered in chapter four, creates a breeding ground where other people's narratives thrive. These narratives, especially ones that try to define your worth, teach you to seek out the approval of others to feel validated, worthy, and loved.

Merriam-Webster defines a people pleaser as

"a person who has an emotional need to please others often at the expense of his or her own needs or desires."

People pleasers derive their worth from making people happy, feeling validated when others approve of them. However, these feelings of worth are fleeting because they are sourced externally instead of internally, so they have to keep pleasing and giving of themselves to maintain a temporary semblance of worth. This is why people pleasing is harmful to their health and mental wellness. It's unsustainable and devours their time, resources, and energy.

If you suspect you're a people pleaser, know it's not your fault. It's a trauma response you've been conditioned to, most likely as a child. You had to adapt to the narratives and gaslighting around you to avoid conflict and consequences. People who people please were loved conditionally and taught to accommodate everyone else's needs in order to be deemed lovable. At some point in your life, you were punished for speaking up for yourself, with shame, guilt, aggression, and exclusion. You were gaslit to believe their version of events which taught you to believe that you had to prioritize others before yourself.

You were taught that your needs didn't deserve any airtime.

Just being aware of any people pleasing patterns you have is a huge first step to ending it. A combination of time and self-awareness will put you on a path to prioritizing yourself and your healing. Freeing yourself from the burden of trying to manage other people's emotions is a massive weight off your back. You will be able to reconnect with the rhythm of your soul instead of the rhythm of others.

It's important to know that many of the narratives you learned did not originate innocently. They were not instilled in you for your best interest. Sadly, many of the narratives that gaslight you were intended to strip you of your power. These narratives were created selfishly to control and manipulate you for selfish reasons such as power, control, and money. Being aware of the intentions behind harmful narratives will help you alleviate any guilt or shame you feel for putting yourself first.

People Pleasing Journal Prompts

Review your daily interactions, outings, and activities. Whatever transpires during your day, reflect on these questions to help you understand if you're unconsciously people pleasing.

- Do you feel guilty saying "no" to others? Why?
- Do you feel responsible for other people's feelings? Why?

- Do you go to great lengths to avoid conflicts? How?
- Do you go with the flow even if it makes you uncomfortable or unhappy? Why?
- Do you feel happy when you do something to make others happy? Why?

ROAD LESS TRAVELED

Choosing to belong to yourself is a lifestyle that often requires you to take the road less traveled. Occasionally your path may look like the highway and at other times it will look like a backcountry road. Sometimes your road will sync up with other people, but the entirety of your journey will be different and unique to you.

Your journey is a culmination of your life experiences. Each experience is for the betterment of you and for your soul growth. You are gaslighting your soul when the external noises and narratives get inside you, influence your decisions, and start impacting your life's trajectory. When you try to follow or copy someone else's path, you and your soul aren't getting properly fed and nourished. You're not getting the life experiences you need that fully and completely represent your soul. Who you are on the inside needs representation if you are to live your life to the fullest as the most authentic version of yourself.

I'll be honest with you. Traveling the road less traveled is not easy, but it's the most rewarding. Some parts of your journey will be hard, while other parts will feel awesome. The more you travel your own path, the more comfortable you'll feel in the driver's seat. Your journey will unfold in perfect timing for your healing and soul reclamation.

There are no wrong turns on your path. There are no mistakes or failures. There are only learning opportunities. Too often people hold themselves back because they're afraid of failure. Some people avoid perceived risks at all costs until they're guaranteed the outcome, when it's no longer a risk and potentially no longer an option for them. There's a time and place to play it safe, but there are also times you should bravely move forward in a new direction even if you don't know the exact outcome. Uncertainty about where your path will lead you is unnerving, but if your gut is telling you to go down the unpaved path, then trust your intuition. This is your best way forward.

What I discovered on my road to healing anxiety is that I didn't have to know the outcome. I just had to take the next step that was revealed to me, one step at a time. When I felt overwhelmed with all of the steps I anticipated I needed to take, I just focused on the next step. Each time my intuition, my soul, and my spirit team guided me to the next step, my confidence grew as I experienced the overall success of my decisions. Eventually, the road less traveled became my only means of travel.

Road Less Travelled Journal Prompts

Traveling on your unpaved path is courageous and will guide you back to your light and soul. The best way for you to travel through your life is by honoring the rhythm of your soul. Take some time to write in your journal about the path you're currently on and where you feel like you're being led.

- Do you choose the well-worn path or your own path? Why?
- Does walking your own path scare you, excite you, or both? Explain.
- What have been the short-term and long-terms results of traveling your own path?

STRUCTURE

You're gaslighting your soul when you're invested in structures that are no longer in alignment with your soul. Structures that are holding you back and keeping your soul freedom out of reach. By structures I mean constructs and frameworks, both physical and abstract, from institutions, constitutions, and organizations. Many of the structures I'm talking about were probably helpful at some point but are now obsolete.

Each day you are in contact with different structures that impact your life. In my own life, I've been able to witness varying structures, some effective and some outdated. An example of an organizational structure is the military. My husband was in the Air Force for 22 years, and I have a lot of respect for the men and women who serve. The military is a long-standing structure and is an exaggerated reflection of our society in that there is a clear hierarchy where the soldiers are labeled and stratified based on their performance and time in service. The purpose for all of the ranks in the military is to create order and structure for clear channels of communication in a crisis. While not perfect, this type of structure works.

Other structures either intentionally or accidentally condition children and adults to become indoctrinated with certain beliefs about themselves. An example of institutional structures are public schools. Public schools are also an extension of society. There are a lot of good things happening in schools, but the actual framework can have long-term damaging effects on children and later adults. It also been my experience with my kids in public schools that there's a lot of corruption where status and money have become the main drivers of the school's administration and some of the teachers. This is sad and frustrating because not only are our children's educations lacking but so is their mental health and emotional wellbeing.

Public schools also stratify and divide kids based on grades, athletic performance, and other standards. They dole out supercilious awards that often reward those who are the teachers' favorites, the ones who play along to an unspoken set of rules. These unspoken rules determine who is "good" and who isn't. From an early age kids understand these rules, and some go to great lengths to bend themselves to fit into the narrow constructs of what's considered "good." In school kids learn to lose themselves and become who the adults and peers around them want them to be.

And then there are grades and GPAs. A letter grade is such a narrow representation of each student, deeming each student as smart, really smart, or behind rather than recognizing each student for their own unique abilities and developing these talents. In school students are viewed as a group where everyone moves at the same pace, instead of having each student move at a pace best suited for them.

When you stop and think about it, how many people actually had a great high school experience? I definitely didn't. My time in high school was traumatizing as I believe it was for most people. I think friendships in high school are more like survival groups where you're forced to navigate this structure and what it feels like to not fit in, coupled with being labeled and stratified into the smart/not smart, talented/not talented, athletic/not athletic, good/bad, and popular/unpopular groups. It's another reflection of the "haves" and "have nots" in society. These narratives start early and last a lifetime for some people. I don't have enough information to say exactly how schools should change, but I know that they need restructuring so that today's children emerge from the school systems feeling empowered, confident, and trusting themselves.

When these structures are all you know, it's difficult to see things differently because you've been programmed this way. But that's exactly what you must do to truly understand what beliefs are your own and which were taught to you and why. Some outdated structures want to dictate your worth based on arbitrary standards, creating division instead of inclusion. Some systems affect how you view yourself and rob you of your power. These outdated structures give certain people power, money, and control when they gaslight your soul and trick you into believing you're not good enough.

"When the institutions that are meant to foster safety betray it and allow remorseless perpetrators to harm others, it's a wake-up call that our systems may support narcissism, sociopathy, and psychopathy rather than meaningfully address and limit them."

— DR. RAMANI DURVASULA, DON'T YOU KNOW WHO I AM?

Sadly, many structures you were taught to trust are outdated and are no longer safe.

RESISTANCE VERSES NON-RESISTANCE REFLECTION

Resistance is opposition you feel on your road less travelled. When you're on your own path, resistance is anything blocking you from where you want to be. Resistance can be roadblocks that are holding you back, pigeonholes that are limiting you, and opportunities that are just out of arms reach.

Experiencing resistance is not a bad thing. As hard and uncomfortable as resistance is, it is ultimately for your growth. When you regularly experience resistance in a certain area of your life it's because there's greatness to come and your soul needs you to level up. The resistance you are experiencing is because the situation you're currently in is no longer working for you.

Many of the situations where you experience resistance involve outdated structures that may have been good for a time but are now holding you back. You could experience resistance at work, at school, at church, a doctor's office, and more. The traditional narrative suggests that there's a problem with you whenever you're experiencing resistance in any area of your life and that perhaps you need to change who you are and give away more of your power. But the truth is it's the situation, the structure, that's not working. You need to go where you are appreciated. When you release outdated structures, there is a reclamation of power on the other side. There is freedom.

For years my daughter danced at an outdated dance studio. As she got older, the verbal abuse at this studio got progressively worse. My daughter is a great dancer, but she was losing her passion for dance and considered quitting altogether. After exploring other options, my daughter now dances at a studio that values her. This new studio works hard to develop dancers while at the same time building their confidence. This studio is run by dance teachers who have come from toxic dance studios themselves. These dance teachers and others like them are redefining the dance world into a more supportive and positive environment, one studio at a time.

"You have to understand, most of these people are not ready to be unplugged. And many of them are so inert, so helplessly dependent on the system that they will fight to protect it."

— MORPHEUS, THE MATRIX

Many people are so invested in these outdated dysfunctional structures that they can't fathom another way. The narratives they've learned are now their own beliefs that they uphold and defend. Hearing about the wonderful studio my daughter dances at, you'd think that the other parents would flock to send their kids there, but they don't. They're convinced that the abusive teaching styles are what will make their children better dancers. Meanness in the dance world is just par for the course. Luckily, it doesn't have to be this way. You can choose your own narrative and choose what structures you want to participate in.

Structure Journal Prompts

Consider these questions to help you decide if there are any outdated structures holding you back. If you think there are, you don't have to decide right away to get rid of them. Take your time to really observe them and come back to these questions frequently to build a case for yourself to eventually make a decision that is right for you.

- Which structures do you participate in that no longer resonate with you?
- Do certain establishments make you feel empowered or disempowered? Which ones and why?
- Do you feel physically, emotionally, spiritually safe? Explain.
- Are you free to express your true self? Why or why not?
- Do you feel seen and heard? Why?
- How do you feel after spending time in one of these structures that impact you negatively?
- How do you feel anticipating going to the structure?

ANCESTRAL PATTERNS

Ancestral patterns are energetic strands that connect you to your parents, grandparents, great grandparents, and further down your lineage. They can be behavior patterns, belief patterns, and/or trauma patterns. If you have anxiety, most likely there are some ancestral patterns that are harming you and which are no longer in alignment with you and your soul.

Not all ancestral patterns are bad and in fact I would say some are good. An example of a good pattern in my ancestral line that I want to continue is our jewelry traditions. My love for nice jewelry comes from my Panamanian lineage. In my family, our jewelry gets shared and passed down with all of the girls and women in the family. My daughter has a bracelet that belonged to my grandmother when she was young.

However, a pattern that is ending with me is the obsession with our appearance (especially the girls and women). The belief that my looks determine my worth was tearing me apart because I never felt like I was enough or worthy. I've had to abandon this belief and relearn my worth for my mental health. I've learned how to source my worth internally and am teaching this new pattern to my children (especially my daughter) for their emotional wellbeing.

Anxiety is a sign that there are dysfunctional ancestral patterns that need to end starting with you. Many people with anxiety are here to clear trauma from their family line. I call them ancestral disrupters. These people are here on earth at this moment in time to end dysfunctional family patterns. These patterns end now.

Disrupting ancestral patterns looks like a row of dominoes set up in a configuration, with each domino positioned to knock down the domino in front of it. Between each domino there's a kinetic energy transfer that keeps the line going. There's a tremendous amount of momentum from all of the dominoes behind you to stay the course. Anxiety is letting you know that it's time to listen to the rhythm of your soul because the path your ancestors have carved out is not for you.

The initial steps you take to break these patterns are the hardest. It's similar to when one of the dominoes is slightly out of line with the domino pattern. If you haven't stepped completely out of the way, there is a tremendous amount of energy and pressure from all of other dominoes on your back. However, each successive step you take to heal ancestral patterns will be easier. With each and every step you take you'll keep moving further away from the energy in that row of dominoes. The farther you get, the less force you will have on your back trying to knock you down, and the dominos in front of you.

Healing ancestral patterns is tough work. You will ruffle a lot of feathers when you reject ancestral narratives and patterns that are dysfunctional. Not many people choose to do this. If healing ancestral patterns is something you choose to do, congratulate yourself for ending the cycle. Because of you, the dominoes in front of you are protected and will still be standing.

Healing and overcoming adversities connected to your family of origin is also taking the road less traveled, choosing to step away from the tendency to do what everyone else did just because that's how it's always been done. Rather than journeying down well-grooved paths created by your family, you are here to courageously break unhealthy patterns. Healing yourself has an exponential effect too, healing future generations in addition to healing past generations.

Healing ancestral wounds often heals us physically too. Releasing the stored energy that is passed down from past generations will heal your body. You heal at a deep cellular level so give yourself the time and space you need. These patterns run deep so be patient with yourself.

Ancestral Patterns Journal Prompts

The questions below will help you sift through the ancestral patterns playing out in your life. Consider which ones are working for you and which ones are hurting you. Be patient and compassionate with yourself as you go through these prompts.

- Which ancestral patterns are present in your life?
- Which of these patterns do you want to release?
- What new patterns will you create?

Connecting to Your Soul Rhythm

Tools to connect you to your soul rhythm will help you strengthen trust in yourself and end the gaslighting of your mind, body, and soul. Everything is constantly changing—your body, your friends, your family, and the world around you, which is why it is important to regularly check in with your soul. What your body, mind, and soul needs at any given time changes, requiring you to pivot and adapt frequently on your healing journey and throughout your life.

The tools below will help you establish a solid connection with your soul. They will help you tune in to your soul and build self-trust enabling you to make choices in your best interest for your healing and growth. Consistently implementing these tools on a daily basis will steadily strengthen and grow your connection to your soul rhythm.

Meditation

Meditation is an excellent tool for tuning into your intuition and soul rhythm. Sitting still in a quiet place helps you to quiet your mind from all of the distractions in your life so that you can hear your own soul and listen to what it has to say. There are many different styles of meditation you can check out online to see what's the best fit for you. The simplest way to meditate is to sit comfortably with your back as straight as possible while focusing on your breathing. Breathe in slowly for four counts and out for four counts. When you breathe in, make sure your belly expands and when you breathe out, your belly flattens. Do this for 10 to 20 minutes every day.

Nature

Observing and connecting with nature is a powerful tool for helping you reconnect to your soul rhythm. Spend time outdoors during the different seasons and take note of the changes you see. Pay attention to the colors, temperature, scents, and sounds around you. Watch and listen to the birds, ocean waves, rain falling, or even the wind blowing. Witness a beautiful sunrise or a breathtaking sunset. There's a rhythm to everything in nature and taking time to appreciate it will rebuild your connection to your soul rhythm.

Diana

The Roman moon goddess, Diana (whom I mentioned in chapter one), is a great ally and can assist you in tuning into your wild side. She's connected to all of the wild creatures at night. She is highly intuitive and completely in sync with nature. Welcoming her as part of your spiritual support team can help you disconnect from people pleasing and tune into your soul. She'll help you rediscover your passions and dial into your intuitive nature.

Writing

Something magical transpires when you put pen to paper (or hands to keyboard). Writing is a great tool to help you hear your own thoughts and feelings, which is why I have journal prompts throughout this book, but especially in this chapter. Writing brings you back into yourself. Instead of reacting to things outside of yourself, you're entirely focused on what's going on inside of you.

Making journal writing a daily practice will really strengthen your connection to your soul. It doesn't have to be much, just five to ten minutes of writing or one page each day is all it takes. I recommend writing down three to four feelings you are currently experiencing as you are writing. This helps you to tune into yourself, your soul, and your intuition. Make your journal practice fun too. Buy funky journals and cute pens that get you excited about writing. If writing by hand is hard for you or you simply prefer to type, set up a file on your computer or phone. Add in some clip art or emojis, color, or patterns to bring the page to life.

Music and Dance

Listening to music is an obvious tool to connect with soul rhythm by allowing energy to move through you physically, emotionally, and spiritually. Moving to music amplifies this connection whether it's dancing, tapping, or swaying. Whatever feels right to you. Feeling music in your soul is an instant connection to your soul's rhythm.

At this point in my healing and writing journey it comes as no surprise that as I'm writing this chapter on soul rhythm, I've also started taking adult tap and hip hop dance classes. My intuition gave me some gentle nudges that it was time for me to start dancing so that I could better teach and write about soul rhythm. Although it didn't make sense at the time, an opportunity came up for me to take dance classes and I followed what made my body feel strong. I'm glad I did because it's been so much fun.

Creating

Everything you create is an expression of your soul. Creating both nourishes and heals your soul while connecting you to your soul rhythm. As you're creating, you shift out of the logical side of your brain and start tapping into your feelings and intuition.

What inspires you? Writing, painting, pottery, making jewelry, dancing, cooking, baking, playing an instrument, and photography are just some of the many avenues you could try. Pick one or two creative outlets that light you up, then commit to doing them at least once a week, but preferably every day. Release the need to have a specific outcome with your creations and just get those creative juices flowing.

DIVINE TIMING

It's important to understand divine timing when talking about the rhythm of your soul. Divine timing is the timing of how things unfold for you—your healing, growth, and the manifestation of your dreams. Divine timing and soul rhythm have a symbiotic relationship, both influencing each other.

It can be frustrating when your healing isn't happening within the time frame you want. This also applies to other goals including financial goals, relationship goals, business goals, exercise goals, and even spiritual goals. Goals are great but you need some wiggle room for God and your spirit team to support you in achieving your goals in the best way possible for you. God and your spirit team have unfiltered vision and can lead you to better opportunities that you may not have even known about.

When someone else has achieved the goal you're working so hard for, it's normal to feel disheartened and left behind. But you're not forgotten. Soul rhythm combined with divine timing is the blueprint for your soul and everyone's blueprint is different. Your blueprints are designed specifically for you with the highest outcome.

Go ahead and take steps to achieve your goals and dreams but release the need for specific outcomes. The big picture isn't always clear, but there's a reason your path is meant for you. Trusting and surrendering to your soul rhythm and your divine timing allows you to go with the flow of your life instead of wasting precious resources trying to swim upstream.

GET WILD

Get Wild is the term I've coined to unleash your untamed wild side—the rhythm of your soul. It's a reminder to allow your soul to step forward and lead the way. Get Wild is about embracing your most authentic self and reigniting your wildest dreams. Trusting the rhythm of your soul means getting in touch with your wild side and setting yourself free.

Your soul craves freedom. Freedom from other people's narratives. Freedom to take the road less traveled. Freedom to abandon outdated structures and the freedom to create more fluidity in its place. Freedom from ancestral patterns. Freedom to reject normalcy and embrace being different and weird. Freedom to belong to yourself first and foremost. Freedom to be who you are, no apologies.

Get Wild is an invitation to reclaim lost parts of yourself— your creativity, your self-expression, your passions, your power, your voice, and your wildest dreams. Reconnecting with these lost parts of yourself will build unbreakable self-trust allowing you to stand firmly in your truth, never again compromising yourself. This is what heals anxiety.

Get Wild Exercise

The energy of the moon, in particular the new moon, can help you connect to your emotions, dreams, and passions. A new moon is the start of a lunar cycle, symbolizing fresh starts and new beginnings. During a new moon the sun and moon are aligned making the moon almost invisible to the naked eye. Sitting outside at night during a new moon will allow you to receive direct energy from it, enabling you to reconnect to your wild side.

During the next new moon, grab a comfy chair, your journal, and a cup of tea and find a safe space to sit outside at night. If you don't have a backyard, just sitting by an open window is also effective. Get comfortable and simply observe the moon and the sounds around you. You can invite the moon goddess, Diana and your spirit team to help you connect to the new moon and tap into your wildness. When you're ready, begin to reflect on the different aspects of your wild side such as:

- What talents or passions have you been hiding?
- What are your deepest dreams that you've put aside?
- Is there something you've always wanted to do if you had the time and resources?
- Which part of you is screaming for attention?

Write all of this in your journal.

Once you've identified what you want, begin to make plans to bring your dreams to fruition. Your dreams and desires can be big or small from pursuing a new career, wearing clothes that showcase your personality, or even just taking up a new hobby. Make your renewed dreams and passions a priority and bring them to life so that you can get wild and live from your heart and soul.

TRUSTING YOUR SOUL'S RHYTHM

Once you've learned to connect with your soul's rhythm, the next step is to learn to trust it. Your intuition is your inner guide helping you build soul trust. It is your internal compass that will ONLY lead you in the direction that's best for your soul. The word intuition has become synonymous with gut feelings because your feelings are part of your intuition. You may feel initially unsure about the cues from your intuition but with time and practice you'll be able to hear your intuition loud and clear.

Wordnik.com defines intuition as "the faculty of knowing or understanding something without reasoning or proof." Piggybacking on this definition, I further define intuition as your body and soul's inner knowing synced up with the universal life force energy that surrounds everyone. Your soul is not just inside you, but throughout you and around you and your body. Your soul knows what is best for you at all times and sends signals to your body about what paths to take and when to pivot on your path. This nonverbal energy exchange from your soul to your mind and body is your intuition.

Much of anxiety stems from ignoring your intuition. Your soul is trying to communicate what's best for you except you haven't been taught how to listen. Interpreting the subtle and louder feelings from your intuition can be confusing at first. With time and practice it will become second nature, and you will instantly know where your intuition is guiding you. When you need to make a decision about something, the best piece of advice I can give you about your intuition is to go in the direction where the path makes your body feel strong. If a path makes your body feel week, that's a no from your intuition. This is a good starting point that's simple as you're learning to hear your intuition.

For example, let's say a new job opportunity has recently come up. Gather all of the information you have about the job, absorb the information, and then sit with it. Feel yourself in that job. Feel it in your body. When you feel yourself doing the new job in your body, where do you feel it in your body? Does your body feel good and strong, or does it feel weak?

Many times, your first thoughts and feelings about people, situations, or events is your intuition. However, you've been taught to ignore these first responses and to talk yourself into a more probable outcome. However, your initial thoughts are the right choice for you. Fully trusting yourself and your intuition means no more second guessing yourself.

Trusting your intuition also means moving forward in a certain direction that feels right for you even though it may not be the logical choice. When you follow your intuition, your soul is tapping into the universal life energy, meaning your soul has access to more energy and information than you may see. Your soul is guiding you based on the big picture which most likely has not been revealed to you in its entirety. So, if the situation or person you're asking about feels good in your body, that's the way to go even if it doesn't make sense. Think of your intuition as your North Star guiding you.

JOY IS SOUL NOURISHMENT

Everything you've learned in this chapter (and book) will allow you to experience more joy because you're honoring yourself and your soul. When you release dysfunction, you'll have more time, energy, and resources for yourself. Letting go of toxic narratives that are holding you down frees you to live your life on your terms and in alignment with your unique and beautiful soul. Getting rid of the noise around you will help you remember your wildness and what brings you joy.

Think back to when you were young. What brought you pure joy? What were you excited to do or see? These are the feelings you want to tap back into again. Good soul nourishment means doing something every day that brings you joy. And what brings you joy each day may be something different such as reading a book, going for a

walk, painting, or snuggling with your dog. Whatever
brings you joy, make it a habit and do it every day.

Joy is hydration for your soul, ensuring there's plenty of
water for your stream to flow. Only a drought can interfere
with your soul's rhythm. Just as any moving body of water
needs water to flow, so does your soul.

Joy is an emotion that has superpowers to heal trauma
and anxiety. As you nourish yourself and your soul with
joy, fear gets elbowed out. The more joy you feel, the less
room there is for fear. Joy is the fuel for your newfound
freedom. The more joy you experience, the easier it will
become for you to identify people and situations that are
dysfunctional. Being able to discern what you do and
don't want in your life will allow you to uphold necessary
boundaries to protect everything you've restored.

6

I WHOLEHEARTEDLY TRUST MYSELF

"Just trust yourself, then you will know how to live."

— JOHANN WOLFGANG VON GOETHE

HAS SOMETHING EVER HAPPENED WHERE YOU THOUGHT "I should have listened to my gut?" Have you experienced an event or situation you had a feeling about but didn't trust? Now, imagine what your life could look like if you completely trusted yourself all the time, a life led from your heart instead of allowing your mind to second guess you or have other influences steer you from your truth. A bold and authentic life is waiting for you when you trust yourself wholeheartedly.

All of the previous chapters culminate into wholeheartedly trusting yourself. Completely trusting yourself is beautiful and powerful. It takes courage and at the same time requires vulnerability. Unapologetic self-trust will dramatically change your life and heal anxiety. It paves the way for you to fully come into your inherent power and embrace it while letting go of the need for approval and acceptance. **Bold Trust** allows you to surrender to and trust your soul's divine timing. True heroism is tuning into your intuition, trusting it, and following your own path.

It takes time and practice to build up the mental fortitude to trust yourself without a doubt since you have most likely spent most of your life ignoring, second guessing, and gaslighting yourself and your inner knowing. Remember, this is not your fault. It's been ingrained in you to abandon yourself. Most people constantly question themselves and seek out the opinions and approval from others. Being told regularly that you're wrong shuts down your connection with your intuition and, subsequently, your soul.

Trusting yourself without a doubt is about listening to your soul, knowing your true north, and following it. Wholeheartedly trusting yourself doesn't mean you have everything figured out. Instead, self-trust invites you to follow your inner guidance with the support of your spirit team about what the next step is and taking it. It's deeply knowing and trusting what's right for you and bravely making the choices that support you. Wholeheartedly trusting yourself is your ticket to freedom.

BOUNDARIES

A big part of the self-care that's required to heal anxiety is implementing firm and loving boundaries. Boundaries protect you emotionally, physically, and spiritually and are something most people haven't learned. Instead, you've been taught to bend yourself to others' needs rather than fiercely protecting your own.

Many people are exhausted because they're overextending themselves to accommodate others instead of prioritizing their own needs. Your life is not your own when you give of yourself to the point where you have nothing left, wearing yourself out physically, emotionally, and sometimes financially. Depleting yourself to provide for others deprives you of the joy you deserve and instead creates and feeds anxiety.

Boundaries are tools to help you prioritize your needs and self-care. They protect your mental health, overall health, time, finances, and energy. Boundaries set clear expectations for what's acceptable for you, creating limits for how you'll be treated or situations you'll put yourself in. They are imaginary lines that when crossed will sound a warning alarm to you that your wellbeing is compromised. Uncomfortable feelings such as anger, hurt, resentment, or frustration can be indicators that your boundaries have been crossed.

Personal boundaries are like geographic boundaries that separate countries, states, and towns. In addition to the physical boundary surrounding a country there are certain characteristics that make each country unique such as language, cuisine, government, religion, and currency just to name a few. Not only do boundaries protect the land and physical space of the country, but they also protect the characteristics that define the country. Like those for countries, your boundaries not only protect you physically but also protect everything that makes you who you are. Boundaries protect your essence so that you are able to heal and thrive.

As you build up the mental stamina to develop unapologetic self-trust and maintain it, you need to create healthy boundaries that support your wellbeing. It's necessary to have boundaries in place to protect your growth as trust in yourself strengthens. Without boundaries, it can feel like you're trying to focus and do work with the TV left on all the time. As you already know from previous chapters, the noise and voices from the TV are loud, constant, and can drown out your voice. Boundaries help you to hear your own voice and embrace your power by removing unnecessary distractions.

Setting boundaries was not something I was taught as a child and didn't learn until I was much older. It's no surprise I had anxiety—I was energetically wide open. I had no boundaries in place to protect me, my space, my mental health, or my energy. From a young age I believed that what I wanted was unimportant. I was taught that my value came from catering to the whims of others. I became hypervigilant to others' needs, initially as a safety mechanism, and continued as an adult out of habit. If I could predict and anticipate other people's needs and moods, I could protect myself from abusive outbursts.

While people-pleasing served me well in my childhood, it was destroying me as an adult. It was a long, outdated trauma response that initially gave me perceived safety. I became so good at reading others that I completely lost touch with myself. I no longer knew what I needed, what I longed for, or what brought me joy. As an adult, I continued to focus on others to keep myself safe, except my diverted attention was consuming me and was no longer keeping me safe because I wasn't taking care of myself. However, I still needed to protect myself, just not through people pleasing.

Thanks to my boundaries, I became cognizant of my own needs. My healing journey with anxiety taught me to tune into myself, my intuition, and my soul. The more I tune into myself, the more I keep my energy in myself. This is self-protection! That's why this book is filled with tools and anecdotes to help you tune into yourself. Listening to yourself, trusting yourself, and caring for yourself are all forms of self-protection. Boundaries provide the much-needed framework for you to come back to yourself, reclaim your power, and nourish your soul. Boundaries will give you the space you need for your soul to breathe again. I have been able to heal anxiety because my boundaries ensure I put myself first. I have learned to become vigilant about my boundaries and self-care.

Spiritual, emotional, and physical boundaries are three different types of boundaries to implement for your protection and self-care. There is not a clean clear cut difference between these three types of boundaries, where one ends and another begins. Rather each boundary overlaps and reinforces each other, similar to a Venn diagram. With clear boundaries intact, you will feel safe interacting with the world without blocking it out.

SPIRITUAL BOUNDARIES

Spiritual boundaries protect you spiritually, leaving room for God and your spirit team to support and guide you. Your connection to the divine is a reminder that you're never alone, keeping you grounded and connected to your intuition. Your spiritual boundaries make room for divine love to lead the way.

The first part of spiritual boundaries is prioritizing your spiritual practice. It's easy to fall out of step with your spiritual practice due to a hectic schedule or when you're going through a tough time. Boundaries that safeguard a consistent spiritual practice allow you to create a solid connection with your spirit team in order for you to receive support from them during challenging times too. A regular spiritual practice strengthens your connection with the divine, making room for your angels to protect you spiritually, emotionally, and physically.

Meditation, going to church, drawing angel cards, using crystals, or reciting daily prayers are some examples of spiritual practices. What you do for your practice is up to you as long as it helps you feel connected to God and is done consistently. When done regularly, your connection to the divine will grow and become stronger over time, which helps to build **Bold Trust**.

The second part of creating spiritual boundaries is protecting your sovereignty. This means claiming your spiritual and energetic independence. If you're like me and have a sixth sense, nighttime can sometimes be a little scary and uncomfortable. I've always been able to feel and occasionally see other spirits and energies around me. Part of my daily spiritual practice is reaffirming my sovereignty. Every night before bed I pray out loud "I am a sovereign being," and then further set my intentions that only God and his Angels are allowed near me and in my house. On those nights when I'm feeling unnerved and don't want to see anything I say exactly that, "I don't want to see any spirits." And it works!

Declaring your sovereignty during your prayers sets a clear spiritual boundary. You are choosing the level of psychic connection you are comfortable experiencing. The key word here is "choice." You have a say in what you experience spiritually since you have ownership of your mind, body, and soul. Your spirit team doesn't want to scare you, so be clear on exactly what you're comfortable with.

Below is a quick five-minute exercise to help you actually feel your sovereignty and the pure strength of your soul. Being able to feel your sovereignty helps you to know how solid you are at your core, allowing you to know in your heart that you are capable of using boundaries to protect yourself. Acknowledging your sovereignty will help you to wholeheartedly trust in your power.

Sovereignty Exercise

Find a cozy spot where you can sit comfortably. Close your eyes and focus on your breathing. Then begin to slow down your breath while breathing deeply. Inhale for a count of four, then exhale for a count of four. As you breathe, feel your shoulders relax. When you feel relaxed, invite your soul to step forward and allow you to feel your sovereignty. Observe what your sovereignty feels like while continuing to breathe deeply. Where do you feel it in your body? How does it feel? Does it feel strong, grounding, or solid? Keep feeling, observing, and breathing until you're ready to open your eyes. Doing this exercise regularly will help you connect to your sovereignty and feel it throughout your day.

As a sovereign being you get to choose what you experience spiritually, based on what you feel is appropriate for you. A simple prayer or conversation with spirit declaring what you are and are not comfortable with will make you feel more at ease with your spiritual connections. Your spiritual boundaries not only impact your spiritual wellbeing but also your emotional and physical wellness.

EMOTIONAL BOUNDARIES

Emotional boundaries safeguard your emotions. They don't control your emotions, but rather give you the space to process them without being inundated with feelings from sources outside of you. As a human living in this world, it is normal to be affected by the people and places around you such as world events, rude coworkers, and rush hour traffic. But if you know your limits and are aware of the people or places that feel harsh and draining, implementing safe boundaries will protect your emotions from being overwhelmed.

The two types of emotional boundaries I'm going talk about, empathic and relationship boundaries, affect people mostly emotionally but physically as well. (Remember the Venn diagram?) These types of boundaries give you room to safely navigate your own emotions so you can heal anxiety. They also protect the solid foundation you're building that's supporting your healing.

EMPATHETIC BOUNDARIES

As I talked about in chapter one, empaths are sensitive to energy from people, places, and things. Therefore, empathic boundaries are about protecting how you feel emotionally and physically, shielding yourself from the overload of energies you pick up on. Empathic boundaries keep your energy intact and prevent you from feeling energetically depleted. When you have anxiety, it's important to build up and protect your energy reserves so that you have the energy and mental strength to heal.

Because you feel just about everything as an empath, it's necessary to implement boundaries to protect your empathic gifts and keep you out of feeling overwhelmed. As an empath you have to be extra selective about who and where you spend time with since you can be easily prone to becoming completely drained due to abrasive energies which can leave you exhausted for days, weeks, months, and even years. Instilling empathic boundaries is about choosing to surround yourself with kind and supportive people and soothing environments and avoiding people and places that overtax your nervous system and deplete you. Learning who and what fuels your energy in a supportive way, rather than drains it, is key to healing.

Harsh energies or situations can't always be avoided, but by limiting your exposure to them you'll be better equipped to handle the occasional difficult circumstance that can't be sidestepped. You'll have more energy and joy in your reserves to cover you during these times. Additionally, there are many subtle things you can do to protect your energy too. If you know you'll be in a difficult situation, carry crystals, orgonites, or some essential oils with you. I find always carrying a water bottle with me helps my energy by ensuring I'm hydrated. Protection prayers (chapter one) are incredibly powerful too. As a sovereign being you can also say before heading out the door that you don't want to feel everything while you're out (spiritual and emotional boundary overlap!). As an empath, you have to listen to what your body and soul needs and give yourself that extra self-care and self-love. Trusting in your empathic abilities and listening to what you need strengthens bold self-trust.

Below is an exercise to help you explore what empathic boundaries you need to implement to protect your energy. Initially you may be unsure about the cause of any subtle shifts in your energy, but the more you observe how you feel around different people and environments, the easier it gets. The key is to remember to keep coming back into yourself and noting how you feel.

Empathic Boundaries Exercise

Observe the people with whom and the places where you spend your time during a day, week, or even month. Think about how you feel in these situations, with these people, and in these places. Pay attention to how you feel before, during, and after certain events such as time spent with challenging coworkers, friends, or family members either in person, over the phone, or on-line. How do you feel in busy and loud places or after scrolling through social media? Do you feel drained, angry, down on yourself, or frazzled?

When you feel anxious, take note of who you were with or where you were at. Be completely honest, there are no wrong answers. What doesn't work for you may be fine for someone else and that's OK. For example, if large crowds make you feel uncomfortable then crowded venues is your boundary. Knowing your boundary, you can plan your outings during times when you know there will be fewer people. Honor yourself and your needs when your friend wants you to go with her to a sold out concert and instead suggest an alternative get together in a setting where you feel safe and comfortable, respecting yourself and your boundaries. Choosing to steer clear of anything that feels harsh and draining to you and your energy is an empathic boundary.

Now, think about the opposite of these harsh energies. What situations leave you feeling fueled and refreshed? Perhaps time catching up with a supportive friend or relative feels good. Does time alone recharge you allowing you to feel centered and replenished? Perhaps reading a book or time spent devoted to your hobby refills you. Making choices that nourish you instead of depleting you supports you and your empathic boundaries.

RELATIONSHIP BOUNDARIES

Relationship boundaries safeguard your mental health and physical wellbeing. They impact both your personal and professional relationships from coworkers, friends, family, and businesses. These types of boundaries prescribe what you need and what you won't tolerate in relationships, making sure your needs are never compromised by trying to meet the needs and expectations of others. Relationship boundaries overlap with empathic boundaries by protecting your energy from draining relationships and situations. They ensure you don't lose yourself in any kind of relationship.

Right now, there are a lot of wonderful messages about kindness, but these messages are confusing. As you know by now, it can be detrimental to your health when you're completely tuned in to what others need at the cost of your own needs. Yes, many people need the constant reminder to think of others but when you have a history of people pleasing, kindness is also a reminder to put yourself first. Kindness is being gentle, patient, and nurturing with yourself. Kindness is taking care of yourself.

Not honoring your needs in your relationships makes you a doormat and takes you even further away from your true self. If you feel like you're often saying "yes" to others when your heart is screaming "no," you're hurting yourself, and in these cases true kindness is actually saying "no." The harsh truth is that some people, no matter how kind and giving you are to them, will never respect you, validate you, like you, or love you. This is why your worth can only come from within you rather than from other people or institutions. This self-acceptance allows to you acknowledge and meet your own needs.

I used to think that if I was nicer to someone who didn't like me, that they would change their minds. This doesn't work and sadly, it's not an act of kindness. It's an attempt to control the situation for a desired outcome and giving when you don't have enough of whatever it is you're giving is not an act of kindness either. It's heartbreaking because you're not taking center stage of your life. Give what you can, when you can, because you can and release any expectations. Say "no" to any and everything that doesn't sit well with you. And for those people in your life who will never see the true beauty of your soul, move on.

Another part of being a sovereign being is that you get to choose who you have a relationship with. For example, just because someone is family doesn't mean they *have* to be part of your life. I know that sounds harsh but who comes into the inner sanctuary of you is your choice. You get to choose.

I had family members coming into and out of my life on their terms until recently. I wouldn't hear from some family for years, and then they would get back into touch with me ready to insert themselves into my family like they had been around the whole time. This didn't feel right to me. However, the noise I was hearing from other family members was that family is family so I should allow these people into my life on their terms whenever they felt like it. I was expected to bend myself again.

Yet when my anxiety got so bad that I didn't want to leave my house, I had to confront these issues in order to heal. My lack of boundaries left me feeling exposed and unsafe in the world, so I began implementing boundaries in my relationships. I started choosing which relationships I wanted to nourish and which ones I wanted to let go of. Even though my intent was not to be hurtful, some people were probably hurt by my choices, but I wasn't willing to sacrifice my own needs anymore in order to avoid hurting someone else's feelings. My intention was to live my life authentically, and I decided that the relationships I invest in must have respect, stability, consistency, transparency, and, for some relationships, love. Wholly trusting yourself means identifying and enforcing relationship boundaries.

Below is a short exercise to help you navigate your relationship boundaries. Most likely you already have some boundaries in place with the relationships in your life. You just might need some additional boundaries to further safeguard you and take your healing to the next level.

Relationship Boundaries Exercise

Allow yourself to be curious about all your relationships. Observe how you feel in the different relationships in your life. Do you feel comfortable or on edge? Are you supported or are you drained? What are your relationship needs? Do you feel safe? Are you seen and heard? Are your needs being met? Is there mutual respect?

Your relationships should build you up, support you, and nourish you. Decide what you need in your relationships and don't settle for anything less. The people who feel threatened by your boundaries are the relationships you should evaluate with a magnifying glass. Those who truly love and respect you will understand and respect your boundaries.

PHYSICAL BOUNDARIES

Physical boundaries protect you physically while supporting you emotionally and spiritually. They prioritize your physical needs so that you can heal, feel your best, and feel safe. Physical boundaries establish clear parameters defining what you need and what you're comfortable with physically, giving you a framework where you can feel safe and grounded interacting with the world around you.

Again, physical boundaries have a lot of overlap with spiritual and emotional boundaries. Your spiritual connection gives you clear insight about which people and environments are healthy and safe for you, enabling you to make informed decisions. Physical boundaries ensure you have the time and space to tune in and connect spiritually so that you can receive this guidance. Your emotional boundaries help you to choose people, places, and situations that are supportive of you, while releasing those that negatively impact your health and mental wellness. Your physical boundaries ensure that you limit your physical exposure to toxic people and situations, protecting your mental health.

Physical boundaries protect your body. They keep you physically safe, defining what people, places, and situations are safe for you. Some examples of physical boundaries that keep you safe include not going out late at night, avoiding places that are dangerous, only hiking with a friend, and locking the doors of your house or apartment.

Your physical boundaries also safeguard whatever you need to feel energetic and at your best, which you need to heal anxiety. Some examples include turning off your phone so you can get good sleep and plenty of it, avoiding certain restaurants because the food will make you feel unwell, prioritizing your alone time so that you can feel recharged, avoiding large crowds and toxic people that drain you, and avoiding any and all physical contact (even hugs and handshakes) with people you're not comfortable with.

If there are people or places that make you feel uncomfortable, edgy, or anxious, then a physical boundary needs to be in place to limit your exposure and physical proximity to them. If other people or places make you feel unsafe, remove them from your life immediately. Some situations may require you to be around someone who is toxic such as at a family or town event. In these cases, have a plan in place and limit your interactions with them. Also establish boundaries about what conversations and activities you will not engage in around these difficult individuals. It does help to put as much physical space between you and that person or group of people. Remember, it's your body and as a sovereign being you get to choose which people and situations you are physically around.

Some people will get upset when you advocate for yourself. Just like with emotional and spiritual boundaries, there may be people in your life who will be bothered when you uphold boundaries for yourself and that can feel uncomfortable, especially when you have a history of people pleasing. However, the people who get upset about your boundaries are the people you most need boundaries for. The people who love and respect you will support you and your boundaries. They want to see you doing well and thriving.

The physical boundaries exercise below will help you navigate the physical boundaries you need. First, you'll explore what you need to feel physically safe. Then you'll determine what you need to feel healthy, strong, and energetic. Your physical boundaries will safeguard these needs.

Physical Boundaries Exercise

I want you to start thinking about the physical spaces where you spend time. Do you feel safe and recharged in these spaces? Are there any changes you need to make to feel safe and secure in these spaces? If they don't feel safe, what can you do to create safety in these spaces or do you need to steer clear of them? Are there any people you need to release who make you feel unsafe? What situations do you need to purposely avoid because you feel unsafe in them? What boundaries do you need to implement for your physical safety?

Next start thinking about your physical needs. What do you need to feel physically at your best? What do you need to feel energetic and grounded? Do you need quiet time to regroup? Do you need to set aside time every day to connect spiritually? Do you need to get out in nature every day? Does spending time with certain friends and family members fuel you? What boundaries do you need to implement to protect your needs?

When healing anxiety, you have to set yourself up for success. There is no more wearing yourself out to the point of exhaustion. Implementing boundaries ensures that you're taking care of yourself physically, emotionally, energetically, and spiritually. You are the priority. Healing anxiety demands that you continually show up for yourself, never again abandoning yourself. Your boundaries solidify the means by which you have built self-trust by this point and for you to become so strong that you wholeheartedly trust yourself.

BOUNDARIES INSTEAD OF WALLS

Sometimes boundaries can become so rigid that they are actually walls. Walls block out the outside world, pushing away people and opportunities whereas boundaries draw a line in the sand allowing us to use discernment to choose who and what we engage with and on what terms. Walls throw you into a vault, boxing yourself in and hiding your true self out of fear of punishment or ridicule. Boundaries are more solid and stable than walls because they are permeable and flexible. They will not crumble and crash like walls. The boundaries I created out of self-love were much stronger and more effective than the walls I had put up out of fear.

People put up walls out of fear, anger, or pain and for good reason—to avoid getting hurt. However, if you're reading this book, it's time to bring your walls down and embrace boundaries instead. Walls may make you feel in control, but they also close off your heart, blocking out all of the love and support from the divine and from people and situations who are supporting you. Boundaries, however, originate from love, specifically a love for yourself.

An example of a wall is when you decide you will never go to another party after a bad experience at a recent one. However, instead you could create a boundary that is a set of parameters you adopt to ensure you're comfortable and your needs are met at the subsequent parties you attend. Your boundaries may include only going to parties for your close friends and family, staying at a party for just one hour, and/or only choosing to go to parties where alcohol isn't served. Choosing to stay at a party for one hour respects your need for alone time as well as gives you time to decompress afterwards. Choosing alcohol-free parties meets your physical and emotional safety needs. Only going to parties for close friends and family fills your need for personal and enriching connections. The difference is you haven't completely shut out parties, only parties that make you feel unsafe, drained, or unsupported. You get to choose to attend the parties that sound fun and fulfilling and decline the ones that make you feel uneasy.

You're erecting walls when you start with *"I'm afraid of ..."* or *"I'm worried about ..."* instead of *"I need ..."* or *"I want ..."* Going back to the party example, never going to another party because you're worried about having no one to talk to or you're afraid of getting hit on by a drunk guy are legitimate concerns. But putting up a wall prevents you from experiencing some fun and intimate gatherings with potential insightful and meaningful engagements. A wall is saying "never." A boundary is saying "yes, but" or "yes, under these conditions."

Knocking down walls can make you feel vulnerable but know that vulnerability is not a weakness. Vulnerability takes courage and strength. It's your vulnerability that allows room for the divine. I call it active vulnerability. You're choosing to be open and vulnerable; you're paying attention and observing the people and events around you and based on what you've seen, you're choosing the people and events you want to engage with. This is wholeheartedly trusting yourself.

While maintaining boundaries requires effort and action, remember that you don't have to do it all on your own. You don't have to become hypervigilant of your boundaries. Be aware of them, follow through with them, and allow room for your spirit team to step in and help you. Your angels will support and guide you with your boundaries. It will take time, practice, and experience to clarify the boundaries you need to support your needs. This is all part of your healing journey.

YOUR VOICE

Your boundaries create space for you to hear your own voice and use it to self-advocate. Trusting your light allows you to be finally seen and trusting your voice ensures you're finally heard. It's essential to your healing to be able to voice your needs and give voice to your soul. Your voice is your ticket to freedom and is the most powerful tool you have in your arsenal.

As you prioritize yourself and embrace your worth, you'll find your own beautiful unique voice. When discussing your voice, I'm talking about much more than your vocal cords producing sound. Your voice is a means for you to express yourself, communicating your needs, wants, feelings, emotions, and even dreams and aspirations. Your voice asserts your boundaries while helping you protect your needs. Your voice will support you in reclaiming your power. Your voice has the power to change the trajectory of your life.

Anxiety brews when you mute your voice in order to keep the peace, to feel safe, to ultimately dim your light. Inside though, your soul is screaming to be seen and heard. Shutting down your voice to keep the peace disrupts and shuts down the flow of energy in your body and your life. This feels awful and is a breeding ground for anxiety. Your soul must be unmuted to effectively heal anxiety. You must speak your truth.

Tune in, listen, and give voice to your soul even when it feels scary. Feathers will be ruffled, feelings will be hurt, but if you have anxiety, it is imperative that you find your voice and use it. Anxiety is a warning alarm that things are not in alignment with who you are at your core and your voice is your tool to set things straight. Part of wholeheartedly trusting yourself is hearing your voice and trusting it.

When you begin your healing journey, your voice may feel small or maybe even nonexistent. However, as you heal and become stronger your voice will also strengthen. Sometimes your voice will sound like a birdsong and other times your voice will sound like a lion's roar. All of these sounds of your voice are good because they represent you and the different facets of your soul. The difference in your voice will depend on the situations and events you're dealing with.

YOUR VOICE AND NARCISSISM

There are people who don't want you to use your voice. These people want to snuff out your voice so that they can live their life how they want even if it means hurting you. These people are narcissists and sadly don't care about you, your health, and your wellbeing. They use their voices loudly and aggressively. Those who scream the loudest or have the biggest tantrums get the most attention, right? But these people are not expressing their soul voices, only their egos. These people create drama and cause harm, expecting the people in their lives to cater to them. It's essentially bullying. These drama con artists demand to be center stage in not just their own life but in the lives of the people they interact with.

Initially, using your voice may feel like you're overreacting because of what you've seen with these drama-fueled people. After years of being quiet and putting other people's needs and wants before your own, it takes time and effort to begin to use your own voice. Speaking up for yourself will upset the toxic people in your life when there's been a long-term pattern of you keeping quiet just to maintain the peace. But with anxiety, maintaining the peace is no longer an option.

You may have had to keep your voice quiet and dim your light for years, or maybe even your entire life, to feel safe. With anxiety your soul is demanding that you advocate for yourself. Your body is flooded with adrenaline, so it is essential to voice what makes you uncomfortable. Say "no" to the places, situations, or people that aren't nourishing you. Back to the large crowds example, if crowded settings make you feel uncomfortable, voice that. Stay away from crowds and voice your need for quieter and calmer environments. Because everyone is unique, with different things nourishing you and different things draining you, it's imperative that you give voice to these differences. In order to break the adrenaline cycle, you must use your voice to ensure that you are surrounding yourself with situations and people who don't spur extra adrenaline. You can no longer put others' needs before your own. Your needs, your health, and your mental wellness come first. To do otherwise compromises your soul's freedom and your freedom from anxiety.

I believe you start finding your voice when you begin to say "no" to any and everything that is not in alignment with your soul. No is a very powerful word and can be a complete sentence. Initially saying "no" may feel difficult and maybe even tortuous, but it gets easier the more you say it. During a dark night of the soul experience, I was inspired to write the section below as I was beginning to find my voice. I hope it inspires you as you find yours.

The Sound of A Woman Finding Her Voice - "NO"

No to anything that's not her truth.
No to invalidation.
No to being silenced.
No to not being a priority.
No to being the scapegoat.
No to always being the caretaker.
No to any narrative that is not her own.
No to being bullied.
No to not being seen.
No to ever feeling less than.
No to dimming her light to make others feel better.
No to people pleasing.
No to dramas, especially ones that interfere with her purpose.
No to generational abuse.
No to disempowering anyone, especially girls and women.
No to the lies she's been told.
No to always explaining herself.
No to being told and believing she is not enough.

The exercise below will help you to start to think about the unique sound of your own voice. It will also get you to reflect on all the times you should have spoken up but didn't. This exercise will spur you to think about how to advocate for yourself with **Bold Trust.**

Your Voice Exercise

If you're experiencing anxiety, it's time to hear your voice and embrace it. This is what your soul is craving. Use your voice to express your truth in a way that feels right for you. Sing it, write it, dance it, shout it, paint it, share it—whatever feels right for you. Fully trust what your body and soul is telling you and voice it!

Think of all the times you haven't spoken your truth. It can be as simple as voicing what restaurant you want to eat at to more in-depth issues such as voicing how you want to spend your free time or where you want to live, work, or go to school. Think of all the ways you've held back. Now think of how you can start to voice your needs so that you never put yourself on the back burner again.

YOUR POWER

Good effective boundaries and voicing your needs and your authentic self paves a clear path for you to reclaim your power, that only ever belonged to you. A power that you may have unconsciously given away by not prioritizing yourself in order to please others, not expressing yourself to keep the peace, hiding yourself to gain acceptance and fit in, or doubting yourself and instead trusting others. Wholeheartedly trusting yourself means reclaiming your power, trusting it, and using it to heal and to live your fullest life.

Your power is intrinsic and is asserted with your voice. It demands that you're seen and heard and that you rightfully take up space in the world. Fully in your power, you start living your own life on your terms instead of how others want to live your life. You prioritize your own thoughts and feelings over the opinions of others. As you embody your power, you become fully centered and grounded in yourself so that you hear your own voice first. You become extremely selective about who you allow into your inner circle in order to keep noises and distractions to a minimum. Just about every decision you make is in the best interest of you, your health, and your mental wellness.

You're embracing your power when you wholeheartedly trust yourself even when nobody else does. In your power, you're free from the expectations of others and are free to express yourself. You're setting the course of your life, making choices based on what you know is right for you even if it's in a direction nobody else is traveling. You're making choices based on what you want to do instead of what you should do. When you're fully in your power, you are the expert of yourself.

YOUR POWER AND GASLIGHTING

The purpose of gaslighting is to make you powerless so that you are malleable in the hands of the gaslighter (the narcissist) in order for them to control you. As a result, most people who have been continually gaslighted become people pleasers. All the gaslighting you experienced has taught you to derive your worth from others, prioritizing their feelings, thoughts, and opinions over your own. Identifying your worth, seeing through the illusions of what's really going on with the people and situations in your life and the world around you, implementing boundaries, prioritizing your needs and voicing them—all of these steps cut through the long-term insidious effects of gaslighting and rebuild solid self-trust so that you can reclaim your power.

When you firmly stand in your power, you boldly and unapologetically trust yourself and can no longer be gaslighted. Maybe it's been a long journey to fully trust yourself and reclaim your power, but it's worth it. All the work you've done to get here puts you in a great position where you know your strength and power and it can never again be stripped from you. You've done the work to build an indestructible foundation. You are stronger and more self-assured than you've ever been. You will no longer be gaslighted and allow outside influences to determine your worth causing you anxiety. This is freedom. This is freedom from anxiety.

You step into your power when you start to say "yes" to yourself. Yes to all of things that used to be a "no." Saying "yes" to yourself feels right and is incredibly freeing. The more you say "yes" to yourself the more natural and second nature it becomes, allowing you to rightfully reclaim your power.

The Sound of a Woman Reclaiming Her Power - "Yes!"

Yes to embracing and speaking her truth.
Yes to living courageously and boldly.
Yes to finding joy.
Yes to embracing her wildness.
Yes to listening to music and singing out loud.
Yes to making time for herself.
Yes to spending money on herself.
Yes to opening her heart.
Yes to knowing she's enough.
Yes to embracing her imperfections.
Yes to being different.
Yes to paving her own path.
Yes to wholeheartedly trusting herself.

Knowing your needs and wants and meeting them is a giant step to reclaiming your power. This exercise gets you to think through your thoughts and actions during the day, helping you to align more with what you want to be doing instead of what you feel like you should be doing. "I should" is really code for "I don't want to." A life filled with a bunch of "shoulds" is not a life filled with joy, integrity, or soul purpose. A life filled with what you want, following your heart and soul, is the only life that will give you freedom from anxiety.

Your Power Exercise

Take some time to honestly ask yourself if your "shoulds" really mean "I don't want to." Taking the word "should" out of our vocabulary will help clarify your priorities. Do you feel like you should have coffee with a friend out of obligation or do you want to have coffee with her because you enjoy connecting with her and catching up? Do you feel like you should go visit your parents even though they constantly guilt, manipulate, or insult you or do you have a loving and mutually supportive relationship with your parents and enjoy your time spent with them? For example, I don't enjoy sitting through three-hour long dance recitals, but I **want** to go to them to fully support my daughter. I am fully in my power when I do something because I want to, and I've stopped wasting my time and energy doing things that I don't want to do.

When you are true to yourself and live your life accordingly, you're showing others that it's safe for them to do the same. You're creating global harmony where there is room for the wide range of unique people to shine brightly. This is what the divine wants for you and for the planet, to wholeheartedly trust yourself so that you can live your life boldly and unapologetically.

AFTERWORD

*"There is freedom waiting for you, on the breezes of the
sky, and you ask, 'What if I fall?' Oh but my darling, what
if you fly?"*

— ERIN HANSON

In chapter one you learned to fully embrace and trust
your emotions free of judgment in order to process them
and listen to what they're telling you. It's with your
emotions that your soul guides you, so you first need to
trust your feelings so that you have the groundwork to
build the other trusts. Chapter two restored trust in some
of your primal needs—food and exercise. Restoring trust
in what you eat and how you move helps you tune into
your body and become centered in yourself. Chapter
three taught you to welcome in divine support and trust it
while rebuilding a solid foundation that is strong enough
to support your healing. Chapter four encouraged you to

trust your light and shine it by knowing you're enough and knowing your worth. Chapter five was about trusting your soul's divine timing, embracing your own narrative, releasing old ancestral patterns, and getting wild. Chapter six was a culmination of all the previous chapters with wholehearted self-trust and how to support and maintain the **Bold Trust** you've created.

If you have debilitating anxiety, it has likely meant the loss of certain freedoms. While anxiety can feel like a curse, I believe it's a gift. It's a wake-up call from your soul letting you know your freedom has been compromised and that it wants to be set free. The root of anxiety is the loss of emotional freedom, freedom of expression, and freedom to define your own truth. This is not only frustrating but damaging to your mind, body, and soul. The dysfunction of this world is felt by people with anxiety; your soul senses something isn't right. When you hear the call of your soul and reclaim your voice, your power, and your freedom, only then will you be fully free from anxiety.

> "You take the blue pill, the story ends, you wake up in your bed and believe whatever you want to believe. You take the red pill, you stay in Wonderland, and I show you how deep the rabbit hole goes. Remember, all I'm offering is the truth. Nothing more."
>
> — MORPHEUS, *THE MATRIX*

There are a lot of similarities between the movie *The Matrix* and anxiety. Anxiety is the alarm that you've been taking the blue pill. Your narrative is not your own and you are living someone else's truth. Now is the time for you to bravely take the red pill, go down the rabbit hole, and see your truth. In the movie, when Neo takes the red pill, he wakes up from a deep slumber and needs time to heal and integrate into his new reality, his truth. And his truth, the real world he's living in, is harsh but he wouldn't change it because the harsh truth is better than living in a lie. It's better to see the truth of what your anxiety is trying to show you and set yourself free from false narratives than to live in a lie.

GASLIGHTING UNRAVELLED

To recap, anxiety is the unconscious and continual gaslighting of yourself to make yourself small in order to accommodate others. Gaslighting is a manipulation tactic making the targeted person question their reality, benefiting the person doing the gaslighting. The source of the gaslighting can be someone from a personal relationship, from a professional relationship, from society, and eventually from yourself. Gaslighting creates confusion, affecting your perception of yourself and your truth. It sadly causes a loss of trust in your own thoughts and feelings. Gaslighting shatters self-trust.

Gaslighting takes away your voice, your power, and your freedom. You're giving away your power to people who will only ever think solely of themselves. Seeing the truth about gaslighting, you're invited to step into your own truth and live your own life. As gaslighting continues to be unraveled, the more you will free yourself from anxiety boldly trusting yourself, reclaiming your power, and unapologetically shining your light.

The general public consensus seems to be that something is intrinsically wrong with people who have anxiety or any other mental health condition. Many people assume that people with mental health issues are the problem. This is so far from the truth and is a form of gaslighting too! My 20 years of experience with debilitating anxiety and then finally healing it has shown me that there needs to be a cultural shift when it comes to mental health and that starts with knowing there is nothing wrong with you.

Anxiety is your body, mind, and soul's reaction to the dysfunctional aspects of the world you live in: the debilitating pace of life; narcissistic, self-centered, and profit driven people; consumerism; the continuous gaslighting, denial, and invalidation from others; superficial ideals and lifestyles detached from nature, wildlife, the seasons, and the planet; lost connections with your breath, soul, body, and mind; detachment from your food, your needs, your wants, and your dreams; a society where the norm is to have frazzled and frayed nervous systems; and severe sleep deprivation. This is why, to heal anxiety, you must implement self-care and self-love in order to ground yourself so that the flaws of this world don't continually upend and rattle you. You must also prioritize deep rest and restoration and give yourself permission to be a human instead of a robot.

FORGE YOUR OWN PATH

Trust that healing is possible and bravely forge your own path. The more weird or unusual your path, the better because that ensures that it is tailored to you and will be specific to your healing needs. With that said, your healing journey doesn't have to be different, as long as it meets your needs. What other people do is irrelevant because what may be working for others may not necessarily work for you. That's why your path is unique to you and is only meant for you.

The beauty of your healing path is that it brings you back to yourself, to your true and authentic self. This is what healing really is—a return to yourself, remembering who you are on a soul level. It's returning to the open, vulnerable, and uninhibited innocence part of yourself. It's discovering your passions and love for life, not caring about what others think. You're freely and boldly taking center stage of your life, ready to set your own narrative and make choices based on your own needs. As you return to yourself and your **Bold Trust** strengthens, you'll see that anxiety didn't define you, but instead it was guiding you.

NO MORE SECOND GUESSING

As you continue to see your truth and know your own reality, you'll stop second guessing yourself. You'll emerge from a place of confidence and deep internal knowing, no longer questioning your intuition or divine guidance.

You'll stand firmly in who you are, moving in the direction of your true north. Rather than ignoring your soul and trying to dampen your light (impossible!), you'll instead listen to and honor your soul, treating yourself tenderly with deep love, respect, and gratitude.

You will no longer second guess yourself regardless of how loud someone is or how many external voices are trying to distract you. When you feel or intuitively know something, you will not be swayed. Your solid foundation, your reclaimed power, and your **Bold Trust** grounds your soul deeply into the earth like the roots of a tree, so that you are unshakable and will never again forget your worth. You have all the answers you need inside you. Undoubtedly trusting your feelings and intuition will forever guide you on your healing path and throughout your life.

NO MORE FOLLOWING

Most of the discussions I hear about social media are centered around who people follow. Honestly, I do it too. People follow social media accounts partly for entertainment and partly for the information they share. Social media as a source of entertainment or inspiration is fine, but it becomes problematic when the voices of who you follow become louder than your own, distracting you from the realities of your own life.

Social media is also confusing when people identify themselves by the people they follow. They talk about their beliefs with respect to who they follow, which keeps people outside of themselves. Undoubted trust in those you follow is dangerous because it prevents you from listening to your own inner wisdom and intuition. Even if someone is sharing accurate and insightful information, it may not all be true for everyone since each person is different. So many people also lie and distort information they share on social media so it's hard to know what the real truth is. It's ok to listen to what others have to say and appreciate helpful content, as long as you're tuned into yourself and can pick and choose what is right for you. Instead, the undoubted trust needs to be in yourself.

Healing anxiety and discovering your own truth requires you to not focus on what others are doing and instead follow yourself. It's detrimental to your mental health to not derive your truth and reality from anyone you follow on social media or anyone else that has a public platform.

Breaks from social media are always healthy for you and your mental wellness because social media can be very distracting and addicting, especially for empaths who feel everything. Try a social media detox for one week, two weeks, or even better for a month to recenter yourself and see how you feel.

MISTAKES

As you are building self-trust and even once you completely trust yourself, mistakes will happen. It's part of being a human. Remember, you're perfectly imperfect. Except, what if your mistakes are not actually mistakes but instead are building blocks to get you from where you are to where you need to be? What if your mistakes are creating a foundation for you to shine your light in the best possible way? Instead of chastising yourself for making mistakes, choose to digest the lessons you've gained from them. Ask yourself what you learned, how you grew, and what part of yourself healed. Rather than viewing your shortcomings as mistakes, shift your perception and see them as learning opportunities that promote your growth. Mistakes are good because perfection can paralyze you and keep you from moving forward.

GO EASY ON YOURSELF

Remember to go easy on yourself. Using *The Matrix* example from above, when Neo takes the red pill and is jolted from the dream, he's freaking exhausted. I'm not sure how long he rests and recuperates, but it seems like it's for a while, perhaps months or maybe longer because he starts off bald and then later has a full head of hair. Healing anxiety takes time too.

Anxiety by itself is exhausting. Your nervous system is on hyper drive, expelling massive amounts of energy making it hard to replenish the energy you've used. Healing anxiety also requires energy to see, learn, and process everything in your life and everything you're going through. As you're healing, you will feel tired frequently because your body is recovering from the huge energy expenditures of having anxiety and healing it. If you feel tired often and don't understand why, please take my advice-rest and then rest some more. You need it! Physically, mentally, and spiritually you are recuperating and restoring. Listen to your body, trust your body, and rest. Keep things as simple as possible to give yourself the rest you need.

KYRIE ELEISON

I got my first and only tattoo of a butterfly when I was 21 and in college. I believe during those college years, my soul chose that tattoo as a way of foreshadowing all the personal transformations that were to come. I often wonder if metamorphosis is painful for the caterpillar and soon-to-be butterfly, because the biggest transformations in my life were incredibly painful. However, my pain eventually alchemized into gold, and my version of gold is freedom from anxiety.

During an especially difficult dark night of the soul experience that I was going through, my angels stepped in to support me with a song from the 80s. A painful experience showed me the depth and dysfunction of my people pleasing patterns. I had to make a choice between doing what I knew was right for myself, my family, and my community, or turn a blind eye to please someone. Knowing I would make an enemy for life was a tough choice for me as a recovering people pleaser.

I chose to potentially stand alone and do the right thing, but I felt guilty for a while because by doing what I knew was right, I was upsetting someone by rejecting their narrative. This experience stripped off my last big chunk of candy-coating shell and I felt raw, vulnerable, and exposed. It might sound strange, but in this deep moment of emotional pain I felt the most connected to my spirit team. One night I felt the need to express this deep loneliness and despair I felt, so I took out my journal and started to write a poem titled *Fully Awake*. I had never written poetry in my life aside from an elementary school assignment, but that night a poem came through me. I've shared my poem below so that it may help you during the dark nights of your soul.

> **Fully Awake**
> *A full moon rising, casting shadows on the ground.*
> *In the darkest of nights, my shadows are found.*
> *No more running, facing darkness head on.*
> *Shocked and scared, my internal marathon.*
> *Time's been wasted, lost at sea.*
> *Waiting for relief, to finally be free.*
> *Fully cracked open, a fresh blank slate.*
> *Vulnerable and raw, now completely awake.*
> *My due north, a path of oneness.*
> *Listen deeply, to my internal compass.*
> *Strengthened purpose, unchartered water awaits.*
> *Clean clear vision, my soul narrates.*

After I finished writing it, I started to hear notes from a song in my head which is how my spirit team communicates with me sometimes. It took me a few moments to realize the song was "Kyrie" by Mr. Mister.

This song was a beautiful supportive message from my angels. *Kyrie eleison* means "Lord, have mercy" in Greek. The lyrics gave words for exactly how I felt, while perfectly describing my healing journey. Words have power and the lyrics of this song reminded me that I was not alone and was loved and supported by God.

On your healing path you will have difficult moments but know these dark nights will pass and they are for your soul's growth and expansion. Even in your darkest moments, you are **never** alone. During your next dark night of the soul experience say "Kyrie eleison" and feel God's presence with you. Welcome support from the divine and let this song be a reminder that God is merciful.

Boldly trust yourself to embrace your anxiety. Listen to and learn what it's telling you and allow it to transform you into the most authentic version of yourself. Allow your anxiety to transform your chains into wings and your pain into gold. Allow anxiety to set you free and be the catalyst that transforms you into a butterfly.

ACKNOWLEDGMENTS

My support crew is small but rock solid and I am incredibly thankful to each of them.

To my publishers at The Good House Publishing for a beautiful, supportive, and empowering experience publishing my first book.

To my book coach and editor, Brette Sember, for your insightful feedback and wonderful writing support. Your expertise and encouragement have helped me grow and develop as a writer. Thank you for helping me see **Bold Trust** to completion.

To my holistic support coach, Kat, for seeing me, hearing me, encouraging me, and believing in me. You have been steadfast in my corner since our first session and have helped me to heal and to learn to trust myself. **Bold Trust** is because of you.

To Noah for inspiring me with your unwavering sense of self.

To Asher for your wild sense of humor.

To Sadie for your bold artistic expressions.

To Marty for your love, support, and for walking this path with me.

To my spirit team for helping me curate this beautiful life.

About The Author

Tricia Easter is a certified health and wellness coach and mental health advocate who's passionate about helping others heal anxiety and destigmatizing mental health issues through open and honest conversations. She writes about her experiences healing anxiety and the truths she's uncovered on her blog at angelsgoldhealing.com.

Connect with Tricia:
www.angelsgoldhealing.com
www.triciaeaster.com
Instagram: @angelsgoldhealing
Substack: triciaeaster.substack.com
Medium: @angelsgoldhealing

Milton Keynes UK
Ingram Content Group UK Ltd.
UKHW050626181123
432603UK00014B/134